JAHB: The Fog Starts to Lift

Mike Spiritfair Marty

Get a JAHB, LLC: Milwaukee

Bibliographic Data

©1997 Michael Scott Marty (Chapters 7-8)
(Completion date: April 21, 2006)

All rights reserved. No part of this artistic expression may be used or reproduced in any manner whatsoever without prior written permission of the author, except in the case of brief quotations embodied in reviews.

Get a JAHB, LLC (Publisher)
Mike Spiritfair Marty (Imprint) is the author and arranger of this particular expression of the Word of God (for antitrust competitive purposes)

Cover art designer (2026):
Interior art illustrator (2026):

Library of Congress Cataloging-in-Publication Data
Names: Marty, Mike Spiritfair, author.
Title: Just another holy book / Mike Spiritfair Marty, BLS, BA, MBA.
Description: Get a JAHB paperback First Edition. | Milwaukee, WI : Get a JAHB, LLC, 2025.
Identifiers: LCCN 2025922292 | ISBN 9798998577369 (hardcover)
Subjects: LCSH: Christianity--History--By period. The Bible--Modern texts and versions. Political science--Political theory--Consensus--Consent of the governed. Law--Religious law in general--Comparative religious law. Language and literature--Literature--Collections--Literary extracts. BISAC: BIBLES / Multiple Translations / Text | LAW / General | POLITICAL SCIENCE / Religion, Politics & State | RELIGION / Christian Theology / History
Classification: LCC BS125-198.B52 M32 2025 V3 | DDC 209.019 M32 V3

First Edition: Has general table of contents but no index

Dedication

Dedicated to Hus and Wycliffe

Introduction

This holy remix of the Christian Bible is about one-eighth the length, and it employs excerpts from nine orthodox versions: King James (KJV), New American (NAB), New American Standard (NASB), New International (NIV), New King James (NKJV), Revised Standard (RSV), The Amplified (TAB), Today's English (TEV), and The Living (TLB).

A "+" has been placed in front of all verses in which one or more words have been changed from the original verse. A "+" has not been placed in front of verses in which only punctuation or capitalization has been altered nor in front of verses in which, for example, "Job" has been respelled as "Joebh," or in which YAH-way, God, Christ, He, or the LORD have been interchanged with each other. Sometimes, though, especially perhaps in the first two sections (History and Poetry), words have been mixed all around and their order changed, though the verse listing is intended to show in what way the words have been rearranged. If there are a lot of verse references for a short verse, presumably the word order has been significantly adjusted to create a particular idea.

Also, Tab 1 is for the setting, Tab 2 is for "God speaks," Tab 3 is for a human speaker, Tab 4 is for the adversarial spirit, and Tab 5 is for a human critic--generally, this is the structure.

This rearranged version is intended not to replace the Bible but to excite people to read their unabridged versions, though, ideally, *Just Another Holy Book* is an improvement in some aspects over the unabridged versions. A condensed work, however, is rarely, if ever, able to match the value of a great original.

Table of Contents

Bibliographic Data 2
Dedication 3
Introduction 4
The Fog Starts to Lift 8
   Vivacity (Viva City) 9
      One 9
      Two 15
      Three 23
      Four 30
      Five 38
      Six 42
      Seven 50
      Eight 58
      Nine 63
      Ten 72
   Tenacity (T) 80
      One 80
      Two--Paul 88
      Three 91
      Four--Paul 94
      Five--Peter 104
      Six 113
   Works Cited 119
      Vivacity (Viva City) 119
      Tenacity 122

Just Another Holy Book (JAHB)
JAHB: The Fog Starts to Lift

-- 2 Esdras 14:47 (TEV)[1]

---
[1] *Holy*

The Fog Starts to Lift

-- *Anna Karenina*, Leo Tolstoy

-- Ecclesiastes 8:11-12
(New King James Version)[1]

---
[1] *Fog*

Vivacity (Viva City)

One

1. These are the facts concerning the birth of Jesus YAH-way: His mother, Mary, was engaged to be married to Joseph. But while she was still a virgin she became pregnant by the Holy Spirit.

2.   And behold, there was a man in Jerusalem whose name was Simeon, and this man was just and devout, waiting for the Consolation of Israel, and the Holy Spirit was upon him. And it had been revealed to him by the Holy Spirit that he would not see death before he had seen the YAH-way's Christ. So he came by the Spirit into the temple. And when the parents brought in the Child Jesus, to do for Him according to the custom of the law, he took Him up in his arms and blessed God and said: "Lord, now You are letting Your servant depart in peace, According to Your word; For my eyes have seen Your salvation Which You have prepared before the face of all peoples, A light to bring revelation to the Gentiles, And the glory of Your people Israel."

3. And the child grew and became strong, filled with wisdom; and the favor of God was upon him.[2]

+4.   As God had said through the prophet Habakkuk: "Here is my servant, whom I have chosen, the one I love, and with whom I am pleased. I will send my spirit upon him, and he will announce my judgment to the nations. He will not argue or shout, or make loud speeches in the streets. He will not break off a bent reed, nor put out a flickering lamp. He will persist until he causes justice to triumph, and on him all peoples will put their hope."

5.   In those days John the Baptist came preaching in

---

[2] *Mary*

	the wilderness of Judea, and saying, "Repent, for the kingdom of heaven is at hand!"
6.	But when he saw many of the Pharisees and Sadducees coming to his baptism, he said to them, "Brood of vipers! Who has warned you to flee from the wrath to come? And even now the ax is laid to the root of the trees. Therefore, every tree which does not bear good fruit is cut down and thrown into the fire."
7.	The people asked him, "What are we to do, then?"
8.	He answered, "Whoever has two shirts must give one to the man who[3] has none, and whoever has food must share it."
9.	When the Jews sent priests and Levites from Jerusalem to ask him, "Who are you?" he confessed, and did not deny, but confessed.
10.	"I am not the Christ."
11.	And they asked him, "What then? Are you Elijah?"
12.	He said, "I am not."
13.	"Are you the Prophet?"
14.	And he answered, "No."
15.	Then they said to him, "Who are you, that we may give an answer to those who sent us? What do you say about yourself?"
16.	He said: "I am 'The voice of one crying in the wilderness: Make straight the way of the

---

[3]*Flickering*

YAH-way.'"[4]

17. Then Jesus came from Galilee to John at the Jordan to be baptized by him.

+18. After this Jesus was led up by the Spirit into the wilderness to be tempted by the devil. And when He had fasted forty days and forty nights, afterward He was hungry.

19. Now when the tempter came to Him, he said, "If You are the Son of God, command that these stones become bread."

20. But He answered and said, "It is written, 'Man shall not live by bread alone, but by every word that proceeds from the mouth of God.'"

21. Then the devil took Him up into the holy city, set Him on the pinnacle of the temple, and said to Him, "If You are the Son of God, throw Yourself down. For it is written: 'He shall give His angels charge concerning you,' and, 'In their hands they shall bear you up, Lest you dash your foot against a stone.'"

22. Jesus said to him, "It is written again, 'You shall not tempt the LORD[5] your God.'"

23. Again, the devil took Him up on an exceedingly high mountain, and showed Him all the kingdoms of the world and their glory. And he said to Him, "All these things I will give You if You will fall down and worship me."

24. Then Jesus said to him, "Away with you, Satan! For it is written, 'You shall worship the YAH-way your God, and Him only you shall serve.'"

---

[4]*Confessed*
[5]*Forty*

25. From that time on Jesus began to preach, "Repent, for the kingdom of heaven is near."

+26. And Jesus began His ministry at about thirty years of age.

27. Now Jesus, walking by the Sea of Galilee, saw two brothers, Simon called Peter, and Andrew his brother, casting a net into the sea; for they were fishermen. And He said to them, "Follow Me, and I will make you fishers of men." And immediately they left their nets and followed Him.[6]

28. When He had gone a little farther from there, He saw James the son of Zebedee, and John his brother, who also were in the boat mending their nets. And immediately He called them, and they left their father Zebedee in the boat with the hired servants, and went after Him.

29. Then as Jesus passed on from there, He saw a man named Matthew sitting at the tax office. And He said to him, "Follow Me." And he arose and followed Him.

+30. Now it happened, as He was dining in Matthew's house, that many tax collectors and sinners also sat together with Jesus and His disciples; for there were many, and they followed Him. And when the scribes and Pharisees saw Him eating with the tax collectors and sinners, they said to His disciples, "How is it that He eats and drinks with tax collectors and sinners?"

31. But when Jesus heard that, He said to them, "Those who are well have no need of a physician, but those who are sick. But go and learn what this means: 'I desire mercy and not sacrifice.' For I did not come to call the righteous, but sinners, to repentance."[7]

---

[6] *Brothers*
[7] *James*

32. "For the Son of Man has come to save that which was lost."

33. "But to what shall I liken this generation? It is like children sitting in the marketplaces and calling to their companions, and saying: 'We played the flute for you, And you did not dance; We mourned to you, And you did not lament.' For John came neither eating nor drinking, and they say, 'He has a demon.'"

34. "When the Son of Man came, he ate and drank, and everyone said, 'Look at this man! He is a glutton and wine-drinker, a friend of tax collectors and other outcasts!' God's wisdom, however, is shown to be true by its results."

35. As they departed, Jesus began to say concerning John: "What did you go out into the wilderness to see? A reed shaken by the wind? But what did you go out to see? A man clothed in soft garments? Indeed, those who wear soft clothing are in kings' houses. But what did you go out to see? A prophet? Yes, I say to you, and more than a prophet. Assuredly, I say to you, among those born of women there has not risen one greater than John the Baptist; but he who is least in the kingdom[8] of heaven is greater than he."

36. "The Law and the Prophets were proclaimed until John. Since that time, the good news of the kingdom of God is being preached, and everyone is forcing his way into it."

37. The following day Jesus wanted to go to Galilee, and He found Philip and said to him, "Follow Me."

38. Now Philip was from Bethsaida, the city of Andrew and Peter. Philip found Nathanael and said to him, "We have found Him of whom Moses in the law, and also the prophets, wrote--Jesus of Nazareth, the son of Joseph."

---

[8] *Demon*

39. For the law was given through Moses, but grace and truth came through Jesus the YAH-way.

40. Now Jesus went about all Galilee, teaching in their synagogues, preaching the gospel of the kingdom, and great multitudes followed Him--from Galilee, and from Decapolis, Jerusalem, Judea, and beyond[9] the Jordan.

41. After this Jesus and his disciples went into the land of Judea; there he remained with them and baptized. John also was baptizing at Aenon near Salim, because there was much water there; and people came and were baptized.

42.   Now a discussion arose between John's disciples and a Jew over purifying. And they came to John, and said to him, "Rabbi, he who was with you beyond the Jordan, here he is, baptizing, and all are going to him."

43.   John answered, "No one can receive anything except what is given him from heaven. You yourselves bear me witness, that I said, I am not YAH-way, but I have been sent before him. He who has the bride is the bridegroom; the friend of the bridegroom, who stands and hears him, rejoices greatly at the bridegroom's voice; therefore, this joy of mine is now full. He must increase, but I must decrease. He who comes from above is above all; he who is of the earth belongs to the earth, and of the earth he speaks; he who comes from heaven is above all."[10]

---

[9]*Andrew*
[10]*Jesus*

Two

1. Now the Jews' Feast of Tabernacles was at hand.

2. About the middle of the feast Jesus went up into the temple and taught.

3. "Strive to enter through the narrow gate; for the gate is wide and the road broad that leads to destruction, and those who enter through it are many. How narrow the gate and constricted the road that leads to life. And those who find it are few."

4. "Do not lay up for yourselves treasures on earth, where moth and rust destroy and where thieves break in and steal; but lay up for yourselves treasures in heaven, where neither moth nor rust destroys and where thieves do not break in and steal. For where your treasure is, there your heart will be also."

5. "Most assuredly, I say to you, he who hears My word and believes in Him who sent Me has everlasting life, and shall not come into judgment, but has passed from death into life. For the Father judges[11] no one, but has committed all judgment to the Son, that all should honor the Son just as they honor the Father. He who does not honor the Son does not honor the Father who sent Him."

6. "Most assuredly, I say to you, if anyone keeps My word he shall never see death."

7. And behold, a certain lawyer stood up and tested Him, saying, "Teacher, what shall I do to inherit eternal life?"

8. He said to him, "What is written in the law? What is your reading of it?"

---

[11] *Constricted*

9. So he answered and said, "'You shall love YAH-way your God with all your heart, with all your soul, with all your strength, and with all your mind,' and 'your neighbor as yourself.'"

10. And He said to him, "You have answered rightly; do this and you will live."[12]

11. But he, wanting to justify himself, said to Jesus, "And who is my neighbor?"

12. Then Jesus answered and said: "A certain man went down from Jerusalem to Jericho, and fell among thieves, who stripped him of his clothing, wounded him, and departed, leaving him half dead. Now by chance a certain priest came down that road. And when he saw him, he passed by on the other side. Likewise, a Levite, when he arrived at the place, came and looked, and passed by on the other side. But a certain Samaritan, as he journeyed, came where he was. And when he saw him, he had compassion on him, and went to him and bandaged his wounds, pouring on oil and wine; and he set him on his own animal, brought him to an inn, and took care of him. On the next day, when he departed, he took out two denarii, gave them to the innkeeper, and said to him, 'Take care of him; and whatever more you spend, when I come again, I will repay you.' So which of these three do you think was neighbor to him who fell among the thieves?"

13. And he said, "He who showed mercy on him."[13]

14. Then Jesus said to him, "Go and do likewise."

15. Then Peter came to Jesus and asked, "Lord,

---

[12]*Lawyer*
[13]*Innkeeper*

if my brother keeps on sinning against me, how many times do I have to forgive him? Seven times?"

16. "No, not seven times," answered Jesus, "but seventy times seven, because the Kingdom of heaven is like this. Once there was a king who decided to check on his servants' accounts. He had just begun to do so when one of them was brought in who owed him millions of dollars. The servant did not have enough to pay his debt, so the king ordered him to be sold as a slave, with his wife and his children and all that he had, in order to pay the debt. The servant fell on his knees before the king. 'Be patient with me,' he begged, 'and I will pay you everything!' The king felt sorry for him, so he forgave him the debt and let him go. Then the man went out and met one of his fellow servants who owed him a few dollars. He grabbed him and started choking him. 'Pay back what you owe me!' he said. His fellow servant fell down and begged him, 'Be patient with me, and I will pay you back!' But he refused; instead, he had him thrown into jail until he should pay the debt. When the other[14] servants saw what had happened, they were very upset and went to the king and told him everything. So he called the servant in. 'You worthless slave!' he said. 'I forgave you the whole amount you owed me, just because you asked me to. You should have had mercy on your fellow servant, just as I had mercy on you.' The king was very angry, and he sent the servant to jail to be punished until he should pay back the whole amount." And Jesus concluded, "That is how my Father in heaven will treat every one of you unless you forgive your brother from your heart."

17. "Your heavenly Father will forgive you if you forgive those who sin against you; but if you refuse to forgive them, he will not forgive you."

---

[14] *Jail*

18. Then He spoke this parable to them, saying: "What man of you, having a hundred sheep, if he loses one of them, does not leave the ninety-nine in the wilderness, and go after the one which is lost until he finds it? And when he has found it, he lays it on his shoulders, rejoicing. And when he comes home, he calls together his friends and neighbors, saying to them, 'Rejoice with me, for I have found my sheep which was lost!' I say to you that likewise there will be more joy in heaven over one[15] sinner who repents than over ninety-nine just persons who need no repentance. Or what woman, having ten silver coins, if she loses one coin, does not light a lamp, sweep the house, and seek diligently until she finds it? And when she has found it, she calls her friends and neighbors together, saying, 'Rejoice with me, for I have found the piece which I lost!'"

19. Jesus went on to say, "There was once a man who had two sons. The younger one said to him, 'Father, give me my share of the property now.' So the man divided his property between his two sons. After a few days the younger son sold his part of the property and left home with the money. He went to a country far away, where he wasted his money in reckless living. He spent everything he had. Then a severe famine spread over that country, and he was left without a thing. So he went

---

[15] *Ninety-nine*

to work for one of the citizens of that country, who sent him out to his farm to take care of the pigs. He wished he could fill himself with the bean pods the pigs ate, but no one gave him anything to eat. At last he came to his senses and said, 'All my father's hired workers have more than they can eat, and here I am about to starve! I will get up and go to my father and say, "Father, I have sinned against God and[16] against you. I am no longer fit to be called your son; treat me as one of your hired workers."' So he got up and started back to his father. He was still a long way from home when his father saw him; his heart was filled with pity, and he ran, threw his arms around his son, and kissed him. 'Father,' the son said, 'I have sinned against God and against you. I am no longer fit to be called your son.' But the father called to his servants. 'Hurry!' he said. 'Bring the best robe and put it on him. Put a ring on his finger and shoes on his feet. Then go and get the prize calf and kill it, and let us celebrate with a feast! For this son of mine was dead, but now he is alive; he was lost, but now he has been found.' And so the feasting began. In the meantime, the older son was out in the field. On his way back, when he came close to the house, he heard the music and dancing. So he called one of the servants and asked him, 'What's going on?' 'Your brother has come back home,' the servant answered, 'and your father has killed the prize calf, because he got him back safe and sound.' The older brother was so angry that he would not go into the house; so his father came out and begged him to come in. But he spoke back to his father, 'Look, all these years I have worked for you like a slave, and I have never disobeyed your orders. What have you given me? Not even a goat for me to have a feast with my friends![17] But this son of yours wasted all your property on prostitutes, and when he comes back home, you kill the prize calf for him!' 'My son,' the father answered, 'you are always here with me, and everything I have is yours. But we had to celebrate and be happy, because

---

[16] *Younger*
[17] *Started*

your brother was dead, but now he is alive; he was lost, but now he has been found.'"

20. "Judge not, and you shall not be judged. Condemn not, and you shall not be condemned. Forgive, and you will be forgiven. For in the same way you judge others, you will be judged, and with the measure you use, it will be measured to you. Why do you look at the speck of sawdust in your brother's eye and pay no attention to the plank in your own eye? How can you say to your brother, 'Let me take the speck out of your eye,' when all the time there is a plank in your own eye? You hypocrite, first take the plank out of your own eye, and then you will see clearly to remove the speck from your brother's eye."

21. "Can the blind lead the blind? Will they not both fall into the ditch?"

22. "No one lights a lamp and hides it! Instead, he puts it on a lampstand to give light to all who enter the room. Your eyes light up your inward[18] being. A pure eye lets sunshine into your soul. A lustful eye shuts out the light and plunges you into darkness."

23. "Therefore take heed that the light which is in you is not darkness."

24. And the Pharisees came out and began to dispute with Him, seeking from Him a sign from heaven, testing Him.

25. But He sighed deeply in His spirit, and said, "Why does this generation seek a sign? Assuredly, I say to you, no sign shall be given to this generation."

26. Now when He was asked by the Pharisees when the kingdom of God would come, He answered them and said, "The kingdom of God does not come with observation; nor will they say, 'See here!' or 'See there!' For indeed, the kingdom of God is within you."

---

[18] *Sawdust*

27. "No servant can serve two masters. Either he will hate the one and love the other, or he will be devoted to the one and despise the other. You cannot serve both God and Money."[19]

28. The Pharisees, who loved money, heard all this and were sneering at Jesus.

29. He said to them, "You are the ones who justify yourselves in the eyes of men, but God knows your hearts. What is highly valued among men is detestable in God's sight."

30. And He said to His disciples, "Therefore I say to you, do not worry about your life, what you will eat; nor about the body, what you will put on. Life is more than food, and the body is more than clothing. Consider the ravens, for they neither sow nor reap, which have neither storehouse nor barn; and God feeds them. Of how much more value are you than the birds? And which of you by worrying can add one cubit to his stature? If you then are not able to do the least, why are you anxious for the rest? Consider the lilies, how they grow: they neither toil nor spin; and yet I say to you, even Solomon in all his glory was not arrayed like one of these. So do not seek what you should eat or what you should drink, nor have an anxious mind. For all these things the nations of the world seek after, and your Father knows that you need them."[20]

31. "But seek first his kingdom and his righteousness, and all these things will be given to you as well."

32. "Do not fear, little flock, for it is your Father's good pleasure to give you the kingdom. Sell what you have and give alms; provide yourselves money bags which do not grow old, a treasure in the heavens that does not fail."

---

[19] *Dispute*
[20] *Barn*

33. Then children were brought to him that he might lay his hands on them and pray.

34. The disciples rebuked them, but Jesus said, "Let the children come to me, and do not prevent them; for the kingdom of heaven belongs to such as these."

35. At that time the disciples came to Jesus, saying, "Who then is greatest in the kingdom of heaven?"

36. And Jesus called a little child to Him, set him in the midst of them, and said, "Assuredly, I say to you, unless you are converted and become as[21] little children, you will by no means enter the kingdom of heaven. Therefore, whoever humbles himself as this little child is the greatest in the kingdom of heaven. And whoever receives one little child like this in My name receives Me; and whoever receives Me, receives not Me but Him who sent Me."

37. "Woe upon the world for all its evils. Temptation to do wrong is inevitable, but woe to the man who does the tempting."

38. "It would be better for him if a millstone were hung round his neck and he were cast into the sea, than that he should cause one of these little ones to sin."

39. "I assure you that whoever does not receive the Kingdom of God like a child will never enter it."

40. Then he took the children in his arms, placed his hands on each of them, and blessed them.

41. And they were astonished at His teaching, for He taught them as one[22] having authority, and not as the scribes.

---

[21] *Alms*
[22] *Millstone*

Three

1. Then He said, "The kingdom of God is as if a man should scatter seed on the ground, and should sleep by night and rise by day, and the seed should sprout and grow, he himself does not know how. For the earth yields crops by itself: first the blade, then the head, after that the full grain in the head."

2. "Again, the kingdom of heaven is like treasure hidden in a field, which a man found and hid; and for joy over it he goes and sells all that he has and buys that field."

3. "Again, the kingdom of heaven is like a merchant seeking beautiful pearls, who, when he had found one pearl of great price, went and sold all that he had and bought it."[23]

4.   Then the scribes and Pharisees who were from Jerusalem came to Jesus, saying, "Why do Your disciples transgress the tradition of the elders? For they do not wash their hands when they eat bread."

5. But He answered and said to them, "Why do you also transgress the commandment of God because of your tradition? Hypocrites!"

+6. "Well did Elijah prophesy about you, saying: 'These people draw near to Me with their mouth, And honor Me with their lips, But their heart is far from Me. And in vain they worship Me, Teaching as doctrines the commandments of men.'"

7.   Then His disciples came and said to Him, "Do You know that the Pharisees were

---

[23] *Scatter*

offended when they heard this saying?"

8. But He answered and said, "Let them alone. They are blind leaders of the blind. And if the blind leads the blind, both will fall into a ditch."

9. Then Peter answered and said to Him, "Explain this parable to us."[24]

10. So Jesus said, "Are you also still without understanding? Do you not yet understand that whatever enters the mouth goes into the stomach and is eliminated? But those things which proceed out of the mouth come from the heart, and they defile a man. For out of the heart proceed evil thoughts, murders, adulteries, fornications, thefts, false witness, blasphemies. These are the things which defile a man, but to eat with unwashed hands does not defile a man."

11. Then Jesus cried out and said, "He who believes in Me, believes not in Me but in Him who sent Me. And he who sees Me sees Him who sent Me. I have come as a light into the world, that whoever believes in Me should not abide in darkness. And if anyone hears My words and does not believe, I do not judge him; for I did not come to judge the world but to save the world."

12. "This is the verdict: Light has come into the world, but men loved darkness instead of light because their deeds were evil. Everyone who does evil hates the light, and will not come into the light for fear that his deeds will be exposed. But whoever lives by the truth comes into the light, so that it may be seen plainly that what he has done has been[25] done through God."

13. Then a certain scribe came and said to Him, "Teacher, I will follow You wherever You go."

---

[24]*Tradition*
[25]*Verdict*

14. And Jesus said to him, "Foxes have holes and birds of the air have nests, but the Son of Man has nowhere to lay His head."

15. Then another of His disciples said to Him, "Lord, let me first go and bury my father."

16. But Jesus said to him, "Follow Me, and let the dead bury their own dead, but you go and preach the kingdom of God."

17. And another also said, "Lord, I will follow You, but let me first go and bid them farewell who are at my house."

18. But Jesus said to him, "No one, having put his hand to the plow, and looking back, is fit for the kingdom of God."[26]

+19. Then He called His twelve disciples to Him. Now the names of the twelve apostles are these: first, Simon, who is called Peter, and Andrew his brother, James the son of Zebedee, and John his brother; Philip and Nathanael; Thomas and Matthew the tax collector; James the son of Alphaeus, and Lebbaeus, whose surname was Thaddaeus; Simon the Canaanite, and Judas Iscariot.

20. He sent them to preach the kingdom of God. And He said to them, "Take nothing for the journey, neither staffs nor bag nor bread nor money, for the laborer is worthy of his wages; and do not have two tunics apiece, and greet no one along the road."

21. "Now whatever city or town you enter, inquire who in it is worthy, and stay there till you go out. And when you go into a household, greet it. If the household is worthy, let your peace come upon it. But if it is not worthy, let your peace return to you. And whoever will not receive you nor hear your words, when you depart from that house or city, shake off the dust from your feet."

---

[26]*Farewell*

22.   "Freely you have received, freely give."[27]

23.   "Go your way; behold, I send you out as lambs among wolves. Therefore, be wise as serpents and harmless as doves."

24.   "Do not give what is holy to dogs, and do not throw your pearls before swine, lest they trample them under their feet, and turn and tear you to pieces."

25.   Now there was a man of the Pharisees, named Nicodemus, a ruler of the Jews. This man came to Jesus by night and said to Him, "Rabbi, we know that You are a teacher who comes from God."

26.   Jesus answered and said to him, "Most assuredly, I say to you, unless one is born again, he cannot see the kingdom of God."

27.   Nicodemus said to Him, "How can a man be born when he is old? Can he enter a second time into his mother's womb and be born?"

28.   Jesus answered, "Most assuredly, I say to you, unless one is born of water and the Spirit, he cannot enter the kingdom of God. That which is born of the flesh is flesh, and that which is born of the Spirit is spirit."[28]

29.   "Therefore I say to you, every sin and blasphemy will be forgiven men, but the blasphemy against the Spirit will not be forgiven men. Anyone who speaks a word against the Son of Man, it will be forgiven him; but whoever speaks against the Holy Spirit, it will not be forgiven him, either in this age or in the age to come."

30.   "It is the Spirit who gives life; the flesh profits nothing.

---

[27] *Twelve*
[28] *Nicodemus*

The words that I speak to you are spirit, and they are life."

31. "Do not marvel that I said to you, 'You must be born again.' The wind blows where it wishes, and you hear the sound of it, but cannot tell where it comes from and where it goes. So is everyone who is born of the Spirit."

32. Nicodemus answered and said to Him, "How can these things be?"

33. Jesus answered and said to him, "Are you the teacher of Israel, and do not know these things?"

34. "No one has ever gone into heaven except the one who came from[29] heaven--the Son of Man."

35. "He who is not with Me is against Me; and he who does not gather with Me scatters."

36. Then Jesus came to a city of Samaria which is called Sychar, near the plot of ground that Jacob gave to his son Joseph.

37. Now Jacob's well was there. Jesus therefore, being wearied from His journey, sat thus by the well. It was about the sixth hour. A woman of Samaria came to draw water.

38. Jesus said to her, "Give Me a drink."

39. Then the woman of Samaria said to Him, "How is it that You, being a Jew, ask a drink from me, a Samaritan woman?" For Jews have no dealings with Samaritans.

40. Jesus answered and said to her, "If you knew the gift of God, and who it is who says to you, 'Give Me a drink,' you would have asked Him,[30] and He would have given you living water."

---

[29] *Where*
[30] *Samaria*

41.	The woman said to Him, "Sir, You have nothing to draw with, and the well is deep. Where then do You get that living water? Are You greater than our father Jacob, who gave us the well, and drank from it himself, as well as his sons and his livestock?"
42.	Jesus answered and said to her, "Whoever drinks of this water will thirst again, but whoever drinks of the water that I shall give him will never thirst. But the water that I shall give him will become in him a fountain of water springing up into everlasting life."
43.	The woman said to Him, "Sir, give me this water, that I may not thirst, nor come here to draw."
44.	Jesus said to her, "Go, call your husband, and come here."
45.	The woman answered and said, "I have no husband."
46.	Jesus said to her, "You have well said, 'I have no husband,' for you have[31] had five husbands, and the one whom you now have is not your husband; in that you spoke truly."
47.	The woman said to Him, "Sir, I perceive that You are a prophet. Our fathers worshiped on this mountain, and you Jews say that in Jerusalem is the place where one ought to worship."
48.	Jesus said to her, "Woman, believe Me, the hour is coming when you will neither on this mountain, nor in Jerusalem, worship the Father. You worship what you do not know; we know what we worship, for salvation is of the Jews. But the hour is coming, and now is, when the true worshipers will worship the Father in spirit and

---

[31] *Thirst*

truth; for the Father is seeking such to worship Him. God is Spirit, and those who worship Him must worship in spirit and truth."

49. The woman said to Him, "I know that Messiah is coming" (who is called Christ). "When He comes, He will tell us all things."

50. Jesus said to her, "I who speak to you am He."[32]

51. And many of the Samaritans of that city believed in Him because of the word of the woman who testified, "He told me all that I ever did."

52. So when the Samaritans had come to Him, they urged Him to stay with them; and He stayed there two days.

53. Then they said to the woman, "Now we believe, not because of what you said, for we have heard for ourselves and know that this is indeed YAH-way, the Savior of the world."

54. Now after the two days He departed from there and went to Galilee.

Four

1. So when He came to Galilee, the Galileans received Him.

2. And Jesus said to them, "I am the bread of life. He who comes to Me shall never hunger, and he who believes in Me shall never thirst. For I[33] have come down from heaven, not to do My own will, but the will of Him who

---

[32] *Worshiped*
[33] *Urged*

sent Me."

3. The Jews then murmured against Him, because He said, "I am the bread which came down from heaven."

4. And they said, "Is not this Jesus, the son of Joseph, whose father and mother we know? How is it then that He says, 'I have come down from heaven'?"

5. Jesus therefore answered and said to them, "Do not murmur among yourselves. No one can come to Me unless the Father who sent Me draws him. It is written in the prophets, 'And they shall all be taught by God.' Therefore, everyone who has heard and learned from the Father comes to Me. Not that anyone has seen the Father, except He who is from God; He has seen the Father."

6. "I tell you the truth, he who believes has everlasting life. I am the bread of life. Your forefathers ate the manna in the desert, yet they died. But here is the bread that comes down from heaven, which a man[34] may eat and not die. I am the living bread that came down from heaven. If anyone eats of this bread, he will live forever. This bread is my flesh, which I will give for the life of the world."

7. Then the Jews began to argue sharply among themselves, "How can this man give us his flesh to eat?"

8. Jesus said to them, "I tell you the truth, unless you eat the flesh of the Son of Man and drink his blood, you have no life in you. Whoever eats my flesh and drinks my blood has eternal life. For my flesh is real food and my blood is real drink. Whoever eats my flesh and drinks my blood remains in me, and I in him. Just as the living Father sent me and I live because of the Father, so

---

[34]*Forefathers*

the one who feeds on me will live because of me. This is the bread that came down from heaven. Your forefathers ate manna and died, but he who feeds on this bread will live forever."

9. These things He said in the synagogue as He taught in Capernaum.

10. And the Jews marveled, saying, "How does this Man know so much, having never studied?"[35]

11. Jesus answered them and said, "My doctrine is not Mine, but His who sent Me. If anyone wants to do His will, he shall know concerning the doctrine, whether it is from God or whether I speak on My own authority. He who speaks from himself seeks his own glory; but He who seeks the glory of the One who sent Him is true, and no unrighteousness is in Him. Do not judge according to appearance, but judge with righteous judgment."

12. "If God were your Father, you would love Me, for I proceeded forth and came from God; nor have I come of Myself, but He sent Me. Why do you not understand My speech? Because you are not able to listen to My word. You are of your father the devil, and the desires of your father you want to do. He was a murderer from the beginning, and does not stand in the truth, because there is no truth in him. When he speaks a lie, he speaks from his own resources, for he is a liar and the father of it. But because I tell the truth, you do not believe Me. Which of you convicts Me of sin? And if I tell the truth, why do you not believe Me? He who is of God hears God's words; therefore, you do not hear, because you are not of God."[36]

13. "If I bear witness of Myself, My witness is not true. There is another who bears witness of Me, and I know

---

[35] *Manna*
[36] *Resources*

that the witness which He witnesses of Me is true. You have sent to John, and he has borne witness to the truth. Yet I do not receive testimony from man, but I say these things that you may be saved. He was the burning and shining lamp, and you were willing for a time to rejoice in his light. But I have a greater witness than John's. And the Father Himself, who sent Me, has testified of Me. You have neither heard His voice at any time, nor seen His form. But you do not have His word abiding in you, because whom He sent, Him you do not believe."

14. "If anyone publicly acknowledges me as his friend, I will openly acknowledge him as my friend before my Father in heaven. But if anyone publicly denies me, I will openly deny him before my Father in heaven."

15. "You search the Scriptures, for in them you think you have eternal life; and these are they which testify of Me. But you are not willing to come to Me that you may have life. I do not receive honor from men. But I know you, that you do not have the love of God in you. I have[37] come in My Father's name, and you do not receive Me; if another comes in his own name, him you will receive. How can you believe, who receive honor from one another, and do not seek the honor that comes from the only God? Do not think that I shall accuse you to the Father; there is one who accuses you--Moses, in whom you trust. For if you believed Moses, you would believe Me; for he wrote about Me. But if you do not believe his writings, how will you believe My words?"

16. "He who has ears to hear, let him hear!"

17. Then he went over to the collection boxes in the Temple and sat and watched as the crowds dropped in their money. Some who were rich put in large amounts. Then a poor widow came and dropped in two pennies.

18. He called his disciples to him and remarked, "That poor widow has given more than all those rich men put

---

[37] *Scriptures*

together! For they gave a little of their extra fat, while she gave up her last penny."

19. "Take heed that you do not do your charitable deeds before men, to be[38] seen by them. Otherwise you have no reward from your Father in heaven."

20. He then addressed this parable to those who were convinced of their own righteousness and despised everyone else. "Two people went up to the temple area to pray; one was a Pharisee and the other was a tax collector. The Pharisee took up his position and spoke this prayer to himself, 'O God, I thank you that I am not like the rest of humanity--greedy, dishonest, adulterous--or even like this tax collector. I fast twice a week, and I pay tithes on my whole income.' But the tax collector stood off at a distance and would not even raise his eyes to heaven but beat his breast and prayed, 'O God, be merciful to me a sinner.' I tell you, the latter went home justified, not the former; for everyone who exalts himself will be humbled, and the one who humbles himself will be exalted."

21. Then each went to his own home. But Jesus went to the Mount of Olives. Early in the morning He came again into the temple, and all the people came to Him; and He sat down and taught them.[39]

22. But when He saw the multitudes, He was moved with compassion for them, because they were weary and scattered, like sheep having no shepherd. "Come to Me, all you who labor and are heavy laden, and I will give you rest. Take My yoke upon you and learn from Me, for I am gentle and lowly in heart, and you will find rest for your souls. For My yoke is easy and My burden is light."

+23. Then the teachers of the law and the Pharisees brought in a woman caught in

---

[38] *Accuse*
[39] *Pharisee*

adultery. They made her stand before the group and said to Jesus, "Teacher, this woman was caught in the act of adultery. In the Law Baruch commanded us to stone such women. Now what do you say?" They were using this question as a trap, in order to have a basis for accusing him.

24. But Jesus bent down and started to write on the ground with his finger. When they kept on questioning him, he straightened up and said to them, "If any one of you is without sin, let him be the first to throw a stone at her."

25. Again he stooped down and wrote on the ground. At this, those who[40] heard began to go away one at a time, the older ones first, until only Jesus was left, with the woman still standing there.

26. Jesus straightened up and asked her, "Woman, where are they? Has no one condemned you?"

27. "No one, sir," she said.

28. "Then neither do I condemn you," Jesus declared. "Go now and leave your life of sin."

+29. Then Jesus came to Bethany, and He went to a Pharisee's house, and sat down to eat.

30. And behold, a woman in the city who was a sinner, when she knew that Jesus sat at the table in the Pharisee's house, brought an alabaster flask of fragrant oil, and stood at His feet weeping; and she began to wash His feet with her tears, and wiped them with the hair of her head; and she kissed His feet and anointed them with the fragrant oil.[41]

31. Then one of His disciples, Judas Iscariot, said, "Why was this fragrant oil not sold for three hundred denarii and given to the poor?" This he said, not

---

[40] *Teachers*
[41] *Alabaster*

that he cared for the poor, but because he was a thief, and had the money box; and he used to take what was put in it.

32. But Jesus said, "Leave her alone! Why are you bothering her? She has done a fine and beautiful thing for me. You will always have poor people with you, and any time you want to, you can help them. But you will not always have me. She did what she could. Now, I assure you that wherever the gospel is preached all over the world, what she has done will be told in memory of her."

33. Now when the Pharisee who had invited Him saw this, he spoke to himself, saying, "This man, if He were a prophet, would know who and what manner of woman this is who is touching Him, for she is a sinner."

34. And Jesus answered and said to him, "Simon, I have something to say to you."[42]

35. And he said, "Teacher, say it."

36. "There was a certain creditor who had two debtors. One owed five hundred denarii, and the other fifty. And when they had nothing with which to repay, he freely forgave them both. Tell Me, therefore, which of them will love him more?"

37. Simon answered and said, "I suppose the one whom he forgave more."

38. And He said to him, "You have rightly judged." Then He turned to the woman and said to Simon, "Do you see this woman? I entered your house; you gave Me no water for My feet, but she has washed My feet with her tears and wiped them with the hair of her head. You gave Me no kiss, but this woman has not ceased to kiss My feet since the time I came in. You did not anoint My head with oil, but this woman has anointed My feet with

---

[42] *Iscariot*

fragrant oil. Therefore, I say to you, her sins, which are many, are forgiven, for she loved much. But to whom little is forgiven, the same loves little."

39. And those who sat at the table with Him began to say to themselves,[43] "Who is this who even forgives sins?"

40. Then Jesus said to them, "When you lift up the Son of Man, then you will know that I am He, and that I do nothing of Myself; but as My Father taught Me, I speak these things. And He who sent Me is with Me. The Father has not left Me alone, for I always do those things that please Him."

41. As He spoke these words, many believed in Him.

42. Then Jesus said to those Jews who believed Him, "If you abide in My word, you are My disciples indeed. And you shall know the truth, and the truth shall make you free."

43. They answered Him, "We are Abraham's descendants, and have never been in bondage to anyone. How can you say, 'You will be made free'?"

44. Jesus answered them, "Most assuredly, I say to you, whoever commits sin is a slave of sin."[44]

+45. "But if the Son sets you free, you will be free indeed."

+46. Then He said to them, "Soon and very soon I will be going away to Him who sent Me. Nevertheless, I tell you the truth, it is to your advantage that I go away; for if I do not go away, the Helper will not come to you; but if I depart, I will send Him to you."

47. "And I will ask the Father, and he will give you another Counselor to be with you forever--the Spirit of truth.

---

[43]*Debtors*
[44]*Bondage*

The world cannot accept him, because it neither sees him nor knows him. But you know him, for he lives with you and will be in you."

48. "And when He has come, He will convict the world of sin, and of righteousness, and of judgment. I still have many things to say to you, but you cannot bear them now. However, when He, the Spirit of truth, has come, He will guide you into all truth; for He will not speak on His own authority, but whatever He hears He will speak."

49. "Peace I leave with you, My peace I give to you; not as the world gives do I give to you. Let not your heart be troubled, neither let it be afraid."[45]

50. "If you love me, you will obey my commandments."

51. "A little while longer and the world will see Me no more, but you will see Me. Because I live, you will live also. At that day you will know that I am in My Father, and you in Me, and I in you. He who has My commandments and keeps them, it is he who loves Me. And he who loves Me will be loved by My Father, and I will love him and reveal Myself to him."

52. "If anyone loves Me, he will keep My word; and My Father will love him, and We will come to him and make Our home with him."

53. "The time is coming when all of you will be scattered, each one to his own home, and I will be left all alone. But I am not really alone, because the Father is with me. I have told you this so that you will have peace by being united to me. The world will make you suffer. But be brave! I have defeated the world!"[46]

---

[45] *Counselor*
[46] *Brave*

Five

1. Then His brothers and His mother came, and standing outside they sent to Him, calling Him. And a multitude was sitting around Him; and they said to Him, "Look, Your mother and Your brothers are outside seeking You."

2. But He answered them, saying, "Who is My mother, or My brothers?" And He looked around in a circle at those who sat about Him, and said, "Here are My mother and My brothers! For whoever does the will of God is My brother and My sister and mother."

3. Then He lifted up His eyes toward His disciples, and said: "Blessed are the poor in spirit, for theirs is the kingdom of heaven."

4. "Blessed are you who hunger now, for you shall be filled."

5. "Blessed are those who mourn, for they shall be comforted."

6. "Blessed are you who weep now, for you shall laugh."[47]

7. "Blessed are the gentle, for they shall inherit the earth."

8. "Blessed are those who hunger and thirst for righteousness, for they shall be satisfied."

9. "Blessed are the merciful, for they shall receive mercy."

10. "Blessed are the pure in heart, for they shall see God."

11. "Blessed are the peacemakers, for they shall be called sons of God."

---

[47] *Filled*

12. "Blessed are you when men hate you, and when they exclude you, and revile you, and cast out your name as evil, for the Son of Man's sake. Rejoice in that day and leap for joy! For indeed your reward is great in heaven, for in like manner their fathers did to the prophets."

13. "Blessed are those who have been persecuted for the sake of righteousness, for theirs is the kingdom of heaven."

14. "But woe to you who are rich, for you have received your consolation."[48]

15. "Woe to you who are full, for you shall hunger."

16. "Woe to you who laugh now, for you shall mourn and weep."

17. "Woe to you when all men speak well of you, for so did their fathers to the false prophets."

18. "Woe to you, scribes and Pharisees, hypocrites! For you travel over land and sea to win a single convert, and when he becomes one, you make him twice as much a son of hell as you are."

19. "Woe to you, scribes and Pharisees, hypocrites! For you pay tithe of mint and anise and cummin, and have neglected the weightier matters of the law: justice and mercy and faith and the love of God. These you ought to have done, without leaving the others undone. Blind guides, who strain out a gnat and swallow a camel!"

20. "Woe to you, scribes and Pharisees, hypocrites! For you devour widows' houses, and for a pretense make long prayers."[49]

21. "Therefore whatever they tell you to observe, that observe and do, but do not do according to their works;

---

[48] *Mercy*
[49] *Scribes*

for they say, and do not do. But all their works they do to be seen by men. They love the best places at feasts, the best seats in the synagogues, greetings in the marketplaces, and to be called by men, 'Rabbi, Rabbi.'"

22. "But you, do not be called 'Rabbi'; for One is your Teacher, the YAH-way, and you are all brethren. And do not call anyone on earth your father; for One is your Father, He who is in heaven."

23. "Woe to you, blind guides! You say, 'If anyone swears by the temple, it means nothing; but if anyone swears by the gold of the temple, he is bound by his oath.' You blind men! Which is greater: the gift, or the altar that makes the gift sacred? Therefore, he who swears by the altar swears by it and by everything on it. And he who swears by the temple swears by it and by the one who dwells in it. And he who swears by heaven swears by God's throne and by the one who sits on it."

24. "Woe to you, scribes and Pharisees, hypocrites! You clean the outside of your cup and plate, while the inside is full of what you have gotten[50] by violence and selfishness. Blind Pharisee! Clean what is inside the cup first, and then the outside will be clean too!"

25. "How terrible for you, teachers of the Law and Pharisees! You hypocrites! You are like whitewashed tombs, which look fine on the outside but are full of bones and decaying corpses on the inside. Even so you also outwardly appear righteous to men, but inside you are full of hypocrisy and lawlessness."

26. "Woe to you, scribes and Pharisees, hypocrites! For you are like graves which are not seen, and the men who walk over them are not aware of them."

27. "Woe to you, scribes and Pharisees, hypocrites! Because you build the tombs of the prophets and adorn the monuments of the righteous, and say, 'If we had lived in

the days of our fathers, we would not have been partakers with them in the blood of the prophets.' Therefore, you are witnesses against yourselves that you are sons of those who murdered the prophets."[51]

28. Then one of the lawyers answered and said to Him, "Teacher, by saying these things You reproach us also."

29. And He said, "Woe to you also, you lawyers! For you load men with burdens hard to bear, and you yourselves do not touch the burdens with one of your fingers."

30. "But woe to you, scribes and Pharisees, hypocrites! because you shut the kingdom of heaven against men. You have taken away the key of knowledge. For you neither enter yourselves, nor allow those who would enter to go in."

31. And as He said these things to them, the scribes and the Pharisees began to assail Him vehemently, and to cross-examine Him about many things, lying in wait for Him, and seeking to catch Him in something He might say, that they might accuse Him.[52]

Six....

1. From that time Jesus YAH-way began to show His disciples that He must go to Jerusalem, and suffer many things from the elders and chief priests and scribes, and be killed, and be raised up on the third day.

2. And Peter took Him aside and began to rebuke

---
[51]*Decaying*
[52]*Cross-examine*

Him, saying, "God forbid it, Lord! This shall never happen to You."

3. But He turned and said to Peter, "Get behind Me, Satan! You are a stumbling block to Me; for you are not setting your mind on God's interests, but man's."

4. "Most assuredly, I say to you, unless a grain of wheat falls into the ground and dies, it remains alone; but if it dies, it produces much grain. He who loves his life will lose it, and he who hates his life in this world will keep it for eternal life. If anyone serves Me, let him follow Me; and where I am, there My servant will be also."

5.   Now it happened on one of those days, as He taught the people in the temple and preached the gospel, that the chief priests and the scribes,[53] together with the elders, confronted Him and spoke to Him, saying, "Tell us, by what authority are You doing these things? Or who is he who gave You this authority?"

6. But He answered and said to them, "I will also ask you one thing, and answer Me: the baptism of John--was it from heaven or from men?"

7.   And they reasoned among themselves, saying, "If we say, 'From heaven,' He will say, 'Why then did you not believe him?' But if we say, 'From men,' all the people will stone us, for they are persuaded that John was a prophet." So they answered that they did not know where it was from.

8. And Jesus said to them, "Neither will I tell you by what authority I do these things."

9. At that time Jesus went through the grainfields on the Sabbath. And His disciples were hungry, and began to pluck

---

[53]*Gospel*

heads of grain and to eat.

10. But when the Pharisees saw it, they said to Him, "Look, Your disciples[54] are doing what is not lawful to do on the Sabbath!"

11. Then He said to them, "Have you not read what David did when he was hungry, he and those who were with him: how he entered the house of God and ate the showbread which was not lawful for him to eat, nor for those who were with him, but only for the priests? Or have you not read in the law that on the Sabbath the priests in the temple profane the Sabbath, and are blameless? But I say to you that in this place there is One greater than the temple. But if you had known what this means, 'I desire mercy and not sacrifice,' you would not have condemned the guiltless."

12. And He said to them, "The Sabbath was made for man, and not man for the Sabbath. Therefore, the Son of Man is also Lord of the Sabbath."

13. And He said to them, "Is it lawful on the Sabbath to do good or to do evil, to save life or to kill?" But they kept silent.

14. "But what do you think? A man had two sons, and he came to the first and said, 'Son, go, work today in my vineyard.' He answered and said, 'I[55] will not,' but afterward he regretted it and went. Then he came to the second and said likewise. And he answered and said, 'I go, sir,' but he did not go. Which of the two did the will of his father?"

15. They said to Him, "The first."

16. Jesus said to them, "Assuredly, I say to you that tax collectors and harlots enter the kingdom of God before you."

---

[54] *Pluck*
[55] *David*

17. Then Jesus told them this parable: "There was once a rich man who had land which bore good crops. He began to think to himself, 'I don't have a place to keep all my crops. What can I do? This is what I will do,' he told himself; 'I will tear down my barns and build bigger ones, where I will store the grain and all my other goods. Then I will say to myself, Lucky man! You have all the good things you need for many years. Take life easy, eat, drink, and enjoy yourself!' But God said to him, 'You fool! This very night you will have to give up your life; then who will get all these things you have kept for yourself?'"

18. And he went on to say to them all, "Watch out and guard yourselves[56] from every kind of greed; because a person's true life is not made up of the things he owns, no matter how rich he may be."

19. Now Jesus and His disciples went out to the towns of Caesarea Philippi; and on the road He asked His disciples, saying to them, "Who do men say that I am?"

20. And they answered, "John the Baptist; but some say, Elijah; and others, one of the prophets."

21. He said to them, "But who do you say that I am?"

22. And Peter answered and said to Him, "You are YAH-way."

23. Then Jesus said to his disciples, "There was once a rich man who had a servant who managed his property. The rich man was told that the manager was wasting his master's money, so he called him in and said, 'What is this I hear about you? Turn in a complete account of your handling of my property, because you cannot be my manager any longer.' The servant said to himself, 'My master is going to dismiss me[57] from my job. What shall

---

[56] *Lucky*
[57] *Manager*

I do? I am not strong enough to dig ditches, and I am ashamed to beg. Now I know what I will do! Then when my job is gone, I shall have friends who will welcome me in their homes.' So he called in all the people who were in debt to his master. He asked the first one, 'How much do you owe my master?' 'One hundred barrels of olive oil,' he answered. 'Here is your account,' the manager told him; 'sit down and write fifty.' Then he asked another one, 'And you--how much do you owe?' 'A thousand bushels of wheat,' he answered. 'Here is your account,' the manager told him; 'write eight hundred.' As a result, the master of this dishonest manager praised him for doing such a shrewd thing; because the people of this world are much more shrewd in handling their affairs than the people who belong to the light." And Jesus went on to say, "And so I tell you: make friends for yourselves with worldly wealth, so that when it gives out, you will be welcomed in the eternal home. Whoever is faithful in small matters will be faithful in large ones; whoever is dishonest in small matters will be dishonest in large ones. If, then, you have not been faithful in handling worldly wealth, how can you be trusted with true wealth?"[58]

24. Now as He was going out on the road, one came running, knelt before Him, and asked Him, "Good Teacher, what shall I do that I may inherit eternal life?"

25. So Jesus said to him, "Why do you call Me good? No one is good but One, that is, God."

26. "But as for your question--you know the commandments: don't kill, don't commit adultery, don't steal, don't lie, don't cheat, respect your father and mother."

27. And he answered and said to Him, "Teacher, all these I have observed from my youth."

---

[58]*Ditches*

28. Then Jesus, looking at him, loved him, and said to him, "One thing you lack: Go your way, sell whatever you have and give to the poor, and you will have treasure in heaven; and come, take up the cross, and follow Me."

29. But he was sad at this word, and went away grieved, for he had great[59] possessions.

30. Then Jesus looked around and said to His disciples, "How hard it is for those who have riches to enter the kingdom of God!" And the disciples were astonished at His words. But Jesus answered again and said to them, "Children, how hard it is for those who trust in riches to enter the kingdom of God! It is easier for a camel to go through the eye of a needle than for a rich man to enter the kingdom of God."

31. Then Jesus said, "A disciple is not above his teacher, nor a servant above his master. It is enough for a disciple that he be like his teacher, and a servant like his master."

32. "You know that the rulers of the Gentiles lord it over them, and the great ones make their authority over them felt. But it shall not be so among you. Rather, whoever wishes to be great among you shall be your servant; whoever wishes to be first among you shall be your slave. Just so, the Son of Man did not come to be served but to serve and to give his life as a ransom for many."[60]

33. Then He said, "The Kingdom of heaven is like this. A man takes a mustard seed and sows it in his field. It is the smallest of all seeds, but when it grows up, it is the biggest of all plants. It becomes a tree, so that birds come and make their nests in its branches."

34. He spoke to them another parable. "The kingdom of heaven is like yeast that a woman took and mixed with

---

[59] *God*
[60] *Needle*

three measures of wheat flour until the whole batch was leavened."

35. Now it happened as they went that He entered a certain village; and a woman named Martha welcomed Him into her house. And she had a sister called Mary, who also sat at Jesus' feet and heard His word.

36. But Martha was distracted with much serving, and she approached Him and said, "Lord, do You not care that my sister has left me to serve alone? Therefore, tell her to help me."

37. And Jesus answered and said to her, "Martha, Martha, you are worried and troubled about many things. But one thing is needed, and Mary has chosen that good part, which will not be taken away from her."[61]

38. And it came to pass, as He was praying in a certain place, when He ceased, that one of His disciples said to Him, "Lord, teach us to pray."

39. So He said to them, "When you pray, you shall not be like the pretenders. For they love to pray standing in the synagogues and on the corners of the streets, that they may be seen by men. Assuredly, I say to you, they have their reward."

40. "But you, when you pray, go into your room, and when you have shut your door, pray to your Father who is in the secret place. And when you pray, do not use vain repetitions as the heathen do. For they think that they will be heard for their many words. Therefore, do not be like them. For your Father knows the things that you have need of before you ask Him."

41. "In this manner, therefore, pray: Our Father in heaven, Hallowed be Your name. Your kingdom come. Your will be done on earth as it is in heaven."

---

[61] *Martha*

42. "Give us each day our daily bread."[62]

43. "And forgive us the wrongs we have done, as we forgive the wrongs that others have done to us."

44. "And do not lead us into temptation, But deliver us from the evil one. For Yours is the kingdom and the power and the glory forever. Amen."

45. Then Jesus said to his disciples, "Suppose one of you should go to a friend's house at midnight and say to him, 'Friend, let me borrow three loaves of bread. A friend of mine who is on a trip has just come to my house, and I don't have any food for him!' And suppose your friend should answer from inside, 'Don't bother me! The door is already locked, and my children and I are in bed. I can't get up and give you anything.' Well, what then? I tell you that even if he will not get up and give you the bread because you are his friend, yet he will get up and give you everything you need because you are not ashamed to keep on asking. And so I say to you: Ask, and you will receive; seek, and you will find; knock, and the door will be opened to you. For everyone who asks will receive, and he who seeks will find, and the door will be opened to anyone who knocks. Would any of you who are fathers give your son a snake when he asks for a fish? Or would you give him a[63] scorpion when he asks for an egg? As bad as you are, you know how to give good things to your children. How much more, then, will the Father in heaven give the Holy Spirit to those who ask him!"

46. And great multitudes went with Him. And He turned and said to them, "If anyone comes to Me and does not hate his father and mother, wife and children, brothers and sisters, yes, and his own life also, he cannot be My disciple. For which of you, intending to build a tower, does not sit down first and count the cost, whether he has enough to finish it--lest, after he has laid the

---

[62]*Pretenders*
[63]*Borrow*

foundation, and is not able to finish it, all who see it begin to mock him, saying, 'This man began to build and was not able to finish.' So likewise, whoever of you does not forsake all that he has cannot be My disciple."

47. And they were astonished beyond measure, saying among themselves, "Who then can be saved?"

48. Then He said to them all, "If anyone desires to come after Me, let him deny himself, and take up his cross daily, and follow Me."[64]

49. "A disciple is not above his teacher, but everyone who is perfectly trained will be like his teacher."

50. "Whoever desires to save his life will lose it, but whoever loses his life for My sake will save it."

51. "For what advantage is it to a man if he gains the whole world, and is himself destroyed or lost?"

+52. Then he said to them, "Every teacher of the law who has been instructed about the kingdom of heaven is like the owner of a house who brings out of his storeroom new treasures as well as old."

53. Then the Pharisees went out and plotted how they might kill Jesus. Aware of this, Jesus withdrew from that place.[65]

Seven

+1. Later He began to teach by the sea. And a great multitude was gathered to Him, so that He got into a boat and sat in it on the sea; and the whole multitude was on the land facing

---

[64]*Build*
[65]*Owner*

the sea.

2. Then He taught them many things by parables, and said to them in His teaching: "Listen! Behold, a sower went out to sow. And it happened, as he sowed, that some seed fell by the wayside; and the birds of the air came and devoured it. Some fell on stony ground, where it did not have much earth; and immediately it sprang up because it had no depth of earth. But when the sun was up it was scorched, and because it had no root it withered away. And some seed fell among thorns; and the thorns grew up and choked it, and it yielded no crop. But other seed fell on good ground and yielded a crop that sprang up, increased and produced: some thirtyfold, some sixty, and some a hundred."

3. "He who has ears to hear, let him hear!"

4. The disciples came to him and asked, "Why do you speak to the people in parables?"[66]

+5. He replied, "The knowledge of the secrets of the kingdom of heaven has been given to you, but not to them. This is why I speak to them in parables: Though seeing, they do not see; though hearing, they do not hear or understand. In them is fulfilled the prophecy of Haggai: 'You will be ever hearing but never understanding; you will be ever seeing but never perceiving. For this people's heart has become calloused; they hardly hear with their ears, and they have closed their eyes. Otherwise they might see with their eyes, hear with their ears, understand with their hearts and turn, and I would heal them.' But blessed are your eyes because they see, and your ears because they hear. For I tell you the truth, many prophets and righteous men longed to see what you see but did not see it, and to hear what you hear but did not hear it."

6. "Listen then to what the parable of the sower means: When anyone hears the message about the kingdom and

---

[66] *Scorched*

does not understand it, the evil one comes and snatches away what was sown in his heart. This is the seed sown along the path. The one who received the seed that fell on rocky places is the man who hears the word and at once receives it with joy. But since he has no root, he lasts only a short time. When[67] trouble or persecution comes because of the word, he quickly falls away. The one who received the seed that fell among the thorns is the man who hears the word, but the worries of this life and the deceitfulness of wealth choke it, making it unfruitful."

7. "But these are the ones sown on good ground, those who hear the word, accept it, and bear fruit: some thirtyfold, some sixty, and some a hundred."

8. "Not everyone who says to Me, 'Lord, Lord,' shall enter the kingdom of heaven, but he who does the will of My Father in heaven."

+9. "And so why do they call Me 'Lord, Lord,' and do not do the things which I say?"

10. "Therefore whoever hears these sayings of Mine, and does them, I will liken him to a wise man who built his house on the rock: and the rain descended, the floods came, and the winds blew and beat on that house; and it did not fall, for it was founded on the rock."[68]

11. "Now everyone who hears these sayings of Mine, and does not do them, will be like a foolish man who built his house on the sand: and the rain descended, the floods came, and the winds blew and beat on that house; and it fell. And great was its fall."

12. And so it was, when Jesus had ended these sayings, that the people were astonished at His teaching.

13. Then Jesus stood and cried out, saying, "If anyone

---

[67] *Calloused*
[68] *Thirtyfold*

thirsts, let him come to Me and drink. He who believes in Me, as the Scripture has said, out of his heart will flow rivers of living water."

14. Then Jesus went into the temple of God and drove out all those who bought and sold in the temple, and overturned the tables of the moneychangers and the seats of those who sold doves, saying to them, "The Scriptures declare, 'My Temple is a place of prayer; but you have turned it into a den of thieves.'"

15. After that he taught daily in the Temple, but the chief priests and other religious leaders and the business community were trying to find some[69] way to get rid of him. But they could think of nothing, for he was a hero to the people--they hung on every word he said.

16. And when evening had come, He went out of the city.

+17. The next morning, as he approached Jerusalem and saw the city, he wept over it and said, "If you, even you, had only known on this day what would bring you peace--but now it is hidden from your eyes."

18. Then Jesus spoke to the multitudes and to His disciples, saying: "Whatever you wish that men would do to you, do so to them; for this is the law and the prophets."

19. "For I say to you, that unless your righteousness exceeds the righteousness of the scribes and Pharisees, you will by no means enter the kingdom of heaven."

20. "Either make the tree good, and its fruit good; or make the tree bad, and its fruit bad; for the tree is known by its fruit. You brood of vipers! how can you speak good, when you are evil? For out of the abundance[70] of the heart the mouth speaks. The good man out of his good treasure brings forth good, and the evil man out of his evil treasure brings forth evil."

---

[69]*Moneychangers*
[70]*Hero*

21. "And blessed is he who is not offended because of Me."

22. "If a brother sins against you, go to him privately and confront him with his fault. If he listens and confesses it, you have won back a brother. I also tell you this--if two of you agree down here on earth concerning anything you ask for, my Father in heaven will do it for you. For where two or three are gathered in my name, there am I in the midst of them."

23. "If a kingdom is divided against itself, that kingdom cannot stand. And if a house is divided against itself, that house cannot stand."

24. And He said to them, "Is a lamp brought to be put under a basket or under a bed? Is it not to be set on a lampstand? Whatever I tell you in the dark, speak in the light; and what you hear in the ear, preach on the housetops. For there is nothing hidden which will not be revealed,[71] nor has anything been kept secret but that it should come to light."

25. "You are the salt of the earth; but if the salt loses its flavor, how shall it be seasoned? It is then good for nothing but to be thrown out and trampled under foot by men. You are the light of the world. A city that is set on a hill cannot be hidden. Let your light so shine before men, that they may see your good works and give glory to your Father who is in heaven."

26. Then Jesus spoke to them again, saying, "I am the light of the world. He who follows Me shall not walk in darkness, but have the light of life." Then Jesus said to them, "A little while longer the light is with you. Walk while you have the light, lest darkness overtake you; he who walks in darkness does not know where he is going. While you have the light, believe in the light, that you may become sons of light."

---

[71] *Offended*

27. "Hear Me, everyone, and understand: There is nothing that enters a man from outside which can defile him; but the things which come out of him, those are the things that defile a man. For from within, out of men's hearts, come evil thoughts, sexual immorality, theft, murder,[72] adultery, greed, malice, deceit, lewdness, envy, slander, arrogance and folly. All these evils come from inside and make a man 'unclean.' If anyone has ears to hear, let him hear!"

28. "Do not think that I came to bring peace on earth. I did not come to bring peace but a sword. For I have come to 'set a man against his father, a daughter against her mother, and a daughter-in-law against her mother-in-law.' And 'a man's foes will be those of his own household.'"

29. "All things have been delivered to Me by My Father, and no one knows the Son except the Father. Nor does anyone know the Father except the Son, and he to whom the Son wills to reveal Him."

30. "'The Spirit of the YAH-way is upon me, because he has chosen me to bring good news to the poor. He has sent me to proclaim liberty to the captives and recovery of sight to the blind, to set free the oppressed and announce that the time has come when the Lord will save his people.'"

31. "The law of Moses says, 'If a man gouges out another's eye, he must pay with his own eye. If a tooth gets knocked out, knock out the tooth[73] of the one who did it.' But I say: Don't resist violence! If you are slapped on one cheek, turn the other too. If you are ordered to court, and your shirt is taken from you, give your coat as well. If the military demand that you carry their gear for a mile, carry it two. Give to those who ask, and don't turn away from those who want to borrow."

---

[72] *Sexual*
[73] *Household*

32. "There is a saying, 'Love your friends and hate your enemies.' But I say to you who hear: Love your enemies, do good to those who hate you, bless those who curse you, and pray for those who spitefully use you. In that way you will be acting as true sons of your Father in heaven. For he gives his sunlight to both the evil and the good, and sends rain on the just and on the unjust too."

33. "If you love only those who love you, what good is that? Even scoundrels do that much. If you are friendly only to your friends, how are you different from anyone else? Even the heathen do that. But love your enemies, do good, and lend, hoping for nothing in return; and your reward will be great, and you will be sons of the Highest. For He is kind to the unthankful and evil."[74]

+34. "Therefore, be merciful and perfect, even as your Father in heaven is both."

35. And then He said, "Be on your guard against the yeast of the Pharisees, which is hypocrisy."

36. "I tell you, my friends, do not be afraid of those who kill the body and after that can do no more. But I will show you whom you should fear: Fear him who, after the killing of the body, has power to throw you into hell. Yes, I tell you, fear him."

37. Then He also said, "When you give a dinner or a supper, do not ask your friends, your brothers, your relatives, nor your rich neighbors, lest they also invite you back, and you be repaid. But when you give a feast, invite the poor, the maimed, the lame, the blind. And you will be blessed, because they cannot repay you."

38. Then He said, "A certain man gave a great supper and invited many, and sent his servant at supper time to say to those who were invited, 'Come, for all things are now

---

[74] *Scoundrels*

ready.' But they all with one accord began[75] to make excuses. The first said to him, 'I have bought a piece of ground, and I must go and see it. I ask you to have me excused.' And another said, 'I have bought five yoke of oxen, and I am going to test them. I ask you to have me excused.' Still another said, 'I have married a wife, and therefore I cannot come.' So that servant came and reported these things to his master. Then the master of the house, being angry, said to his servant, 'Go out quickly into the streets and lanes of the city, and bring in here the poor and the maimed and the lame and the blind.' And the servant said, 'Master, it is done as you commanded, and still there is room.' Then the master said to the servant, 'Go out into the highways and hedges, and compel them to come in, that my house may be filled.'"

39. So Jesus said to them, "Everyone to whom much is given, from him much will be required. And everyone who has left houses or brothers or sisters or father or mother or wife or children or lands, for My name's sake, shall receive a hundredfold, and inherit everlasting life. And behold, some are last who will be first and some are first who will be last."[76]

40. Now some of them wanted to take Him, but no one laid hands on Him.

41. Then the officers came to the chief priests and Pharisees, who said to them, "Why have you not brought Him?"

42. The officers answered, "No man ever spoke like this Man!"

43. Then the Pharisees answered them, "Are you also deceived?"

44. Then He left them and went out of the city to Bethany, and

---

[75] *Hypocrisy*
[76] *Excused*

He lodged there.

Eight

1. Now in the morning, as He returned to the city, He was hungry. And seeing a fig tree by the road, He came to it and found nothing on it but leaves, and said to it, "Let no fruit grow on you ever again." And immediately the fig tree withered away.[77]

2. Now when the disciples saw it, they marveled, saying, "How did the fig tree wither away so soon?"

3. So Jesus answered and said to them, "Assuredly, I say to you, if you have faith and do not doubt, you will not only do what was done to the fig tree, but also if you say to this mountain, 'Be removed and be cast into the sea,' it will be done."

4. Then the Pharisees and Sadducees came, and testing Him asked that He would show them a sign from heaven.

5. He answered and said to them, "When you see a cloud rising out of the west, immediately you say, 'A shower is coming'; and so it is. And when you see the south wind blow, you say, 'There will be hot weather'; and there is." Then He also said, "When it is evening you say, 'It will be fair weather, for the sky is red'; and in the morning, 'It will be foul weather today, for the sky is red and threatening.' Hypocrites! You know how to discern the face of the sky, but you cannot discern the signs of the times."[78]

6. Then the Pharisees went out and laid plans to trap him in his words. "Teacher," they

---

[77] *Chief*
[78] *Wither*

said, "we know you are a man of integrity and that you teach the way of God in accordance with the truth. You aren't swayed by men, because you pay no attention to who they are. Tell us then, what is your opinion? Is it right to pay taxes to Caesar or not?"

7. Jesus replied, "Show me the coin used for paying the tax." They brought him a denarius, and he asked them, "Whose portrait is this? And whose inscription?"

8.   "Caesar's," they replied.

9. Then he said to them, "Give to Caesar what is Caesar's, and to God what is God's."

10. His reply surprised and baffled them and they went away.

11. Then, with the crowds listening, he turned to his disciples and said, "I am the true vine, and My Father is the vinedresser. Every branch in Me that does not bear fruit He takes away; and every branch that bears[79] fruit He prunes, that it may bear more fruit. Abide in Me, and I in you. As the branch cannot bear fruit of itself, unless it abides in the vine, neither can you, unless you abide in Me. I am the vine, you are the branches. He who abides in Me, and I in him, bears much fruit; for without Me you can do nothing. If anyone does not abide in Me, he is cast out as a branch and is withered; and they gather them and throw them into the fire, and they are burned. By this My Father is glorified, that you bear much fruit."

12. "If the world hates you, you know that it hated Me before it hated you."

13. "Therefore, beware of men; for they will deliver you up to councils, and flog you in their synagogues, and you will be dragged before governors and kings for my sake,

---

[79]*Caesar*

to bear testimony before them and the Gentiles."

14. "When they deliver you up, do not be anxious how you are to speak or what you are to say; for what you are to say will be given to you in that hour; for it is not you who speak, but the Spirit of your Father speaking through you."[80]

15. "If you were of the world, the world would love its own. Yet because you are not of the world, but I chose you out of the world, therefore the world hates you. Remember the word that I said to you, 'A servant is not greater than his master.' If they persecuted Me, they will also persecute you. If they kept My word, they will keep yours also. But all these things they will do to you for My name's sake, because they do not know Him who sent Me. If I had not come and spoken to them, they would have no sin, but now they have no excuse for their sin."

16. "These things I have spoken to you, that you should not be made to stumble. They will put you out of the synagogues; yes, the time is coming that whoever kills you will think that he offers God service. And these things they will do to you because they have not known the Father nor Me."

17. "You have heard that people were told in the past, 'Do not commit murder; anyone who does will be brought to trial.' But now I tell you: whoever is angry with his brother will be brought to trial, whoever calls his brother 'You good-for-nothing!' will be brought before the Council, and whoever calls his brother a worthless fool will be in danger of going[81] to the fire of hell. So if you are about to offer your gift to God at the altar and there you remember that your brother has something against you, leave your gift there in front of the altar, go at once and make peace with your brother, and then come back and offer your gift to God."

---

[80] *Dragged*
[81] *Good-for-nothing*

18. "And whenever you stand praying, if you have anything against anyone, forgive him, that your Father in heaven may also forgive you your trespasses. But if you do not forgive, neither will your Father in heaven forgive your trespasses."

19. "You have also heard that people were told in the past, 'Do not break your promise, but do what you have vowed to the Lord to do.' But now I tell you: do not use any vow when you make a promise. Just say 'Yes' or 'No'--anything else you say comes from the Evil One."

20. "It was also said, 'Anyone who divorces his wife must give her a written notice of divorce.' But now I tell you: When a man divorces his wife to marry someone else, he commits adultery against her. And if a wife divorces her husband and remarries, she, too, commits adultery."[82]

+21. Some Pharisees came and asked him, "Do you then not permit divorce?"

22. "What did Moses say about divorce?" Jesus asked them.

23. "He said it was all right," they replied.

24. "And why did he say that?" Jesus asked. "I'll tell you why--it was a concession to your hardhearted wickedness. But it certainly isn't God's way. For from the very first he made man and woman to be joined together permanently in marriage; therefore, a man is to leave his father and mother, and he and his wife are united so that they are no longer two, but one. And no man may separate what God has joined together."

25. The disciples said to him, "If this is the situation between a husband and wife, it is better not to marry."

26. Jesus replied, "You have heard that it was said, 'Do not

---

[82] *Yes*

commit adultery.' But now I tell you: anyone who looks at a woman and wants to possess her is guilty of committing adultery with her in his heart."[83]

27. "So if your hand causes you to sin, cut it off. And if your foot causes you to sin, cut it off. And if your eye causes you to sin, pluck it out. It is better for you to enter the kingdom of God with one eye than to have two eyes and be thrown into hell."

28. "Not everyone can accept this word, but only those to whom it has been given. For some are eunuchs because they were born that way; others were made that way by men; and others have renounced marriage because of the kingdom of heaven. The one who can accept this should accept it."

29.   Then the Sadducees, who say there is no resurrection, came to him with a question. "Teacher," they said, "Moses wrote for us that if a man's brother dies and leaves a wife but no children, the man must marry the widow and have children for his brother. Now there were seven brothers. The first one married and died without leaving any children. The second one married the widow, but he also died, leaving no child. It was the same with the third. In fact, none of the seven left any children. Last of all, the woman died too. At the resurrection whose wife will she be, since the seven were married to her?"[84]

+30. Jesus replied, "Are you not in error because you do not know the Scriptures or the power of God? When the dead rise, they will neither marry nor be given in marriage; they will be like the angels in heaven. Now about the dead rising--have you not read in the book of Daniel, in the account of the bush, how God said to him,

---

[83] *Hardhearted*
[84] *Accept*

'I am the God of Jehoshaphat, the God of Jonah, and the God of David'? He is not the God of the dead, but of the living. You are badly mistaken!"

31. One of the teachers of the law came and heard them debating. Noticing that Jesus had given them a good answer, he asked him, "Of all the commandments, which is the most important?"

32. "The most important one," answered Jesus, "is this: 'Hear, O Israel, YAH-way our God, the Lord is one. Love the Lord your God with all your heart and with all your soul and with all your mind and with all your strength.' The second is this: 'Love your neighbor as yourself.' There is no commandment greater than these."

33. "Well said, teacher," the man replied. "You are right in saying that God is one and there is no other but him. To love him with all your heart,[85] with all your understanding and with all your strength, and to love your neighbor as yourself is more important than all burnt offerings and sacrifices."

34. When Jesus saw that he had answered wisely, he said to him, "You are not far from the kingdom of God."

35. And from then on no one dared ask him any more questions.

Nine

1. It was now the day before the Passover Festival. Jesus knew that the hour had come for him to leave this world and go to the Father. He had always loved those in the world who were his own, and he loved them to the very end. Jesus knew that the Father had given him complete power; he knew that

---

[85]*Important*

he had come from God and was going to God.

2. So he rose from the table, took off his outer garment, and tied a towel[86] around his waist. Then he poured some water into a washbasin and began to wash the disciples' feet and dry them with the towel around his waist.

3. He came to Simon Peter, who said to him, "Are you going to wash my feet, Lord?"

4. Jesus answered him, "You do not understand now what I am doing, but you will understand later."

5. Peter declared, "Never at any time will you wash my feet!"

6. "If I do not wash your feet," Jesus answered, "you will no longer be my disciple."

7. After Jesus had washed their feet, he put his outer garment back on and returned to his place at the table. "Do you understand what I have just done to you?" he asked. "You call me Teacher and Lord, and it is right that you do so, because that is what I am. I, your Lord and Teacher, have just washed your feet. You, then, should wash one[87] another's feet. I have set an example for you, so that you will do just what I have done for you. I am telling you the truth: no slave is greater than his master, and no messenger is greater than the one who sent him. Now that you know this truth, how happy you will be if you put it into practice!"

8. "Little children, I shall be with you a little while longer. You will seek Me; and as I said to the Jews, 'Where I am going, you cannot come,' so now I say to you. A new commandment I give to you, that you love one another; as I have loved you, that you also love one another. By this all will know that you are My disciples, if you have love for one another."

---

[86]*Passover*
[87]*Washbasin*

9. "As the Father loved Me, I also have loved you; abide in My love. If you keep My commandments, you will abide in My love, just as I have kept My Father's commandments and abide in His love. These things I have spoken to you, that My joy may remain in you, and that your joy may be full."

10. "Greater love has no one than this, than to lay down one's life for his[88] friends. You are My friends if you do whatever I command you. No longer do I call you servants, for a servant does not know what his master is doing; but I have called you friends, for all things that I heard from My Father I have made known to you."

11. "This is My commandment, that you love one another as I have loved you."

12. Then He told a parable: "When you are invited by anyone to a wedding feast, do not sit down in the best place, lest one more honorable than you be invited, and the host who invited both of you may approach you and say, 'Give your place to this man,' and then you would proceed with embarrassment to take the lowest place. Rather, when you are invited, go and take the lowest place so that when the host comes to you he may say, 'My friend, move up to a higher position.' Then you will enjoy the esteem of your companions at the table. For everyone who exalts himself will be humbled, but the one who humbles himself will be exalted."

13. "The Kingdom of Heaven can be illustrated by the story of ten[89] bridesmaids who took their lamps and went to meet the bridegroom. But only five of them were wise enough to fill their lamps with oil, while the other five were foolish and forgot. So, when the bridegroom was delayed, they lay down to rest until midnight, when they were roused by the shout, 'The bridegroom is coming!

---

[88]*Messenger*
[89]*Invited*

Come out and welcome him!' All the girls jumped up and trimmed their lamps. Then the five who hadn't any oil begged the others to share with them, for their lamps were going out. But the others replied, 'We haven't enough. Go instead to the shops and buy some for yourselves.' But while they were gone, the bridegroom came, and those who were ready went in with him to the marriage feast, and the door was locked. Later, when the other five returned, they stood outside, calling, 'Sir, open the door for us!' But he called back, 'Go away! It is too late!'"

14. "For as the lightning comes from the east and flashes to the west, so also will the coming of the Son of Man be. No one knows, however, when that day and hour will come--neither the angels in heaven nor the Son; the Father alone knows. The coming of the Son of Man will be like what happened in the time of Noah. In the days before the flood people ate and drank, men and women married, up to the very day[90] Noah went into the boat; yet they did not realize what was happening until the flood came and swept them all away. That is how it will be when the Son of Man comes."

15. Then Jesus said to them, "See that no one deceives you. Many false prophets will arise; and because of the

---

[90] *Lightning*

increase of evildoing, the love of many will grow cold. But the one who perseveres to the end will be saved."

16. "Be on the alert then, for you do not know the day nor the hour."

17. "Again, the kingdom of heaven is like a landowner who went out early in the morning to hire laborers for his vineyard. Now when he had agreed with the laborers for a denarius a day, he sent them into his vineyard. And he went out about the third hour and saw others standing idle in the marketplace, and said to them, 'You also go into the vineyard, and whatever is right I will give you.' And they went. Again he went out about the sixth and the ninth hour, and did likewise. And about the eleventh hour he went out and found others standing idle, and said to them, 'Why have you been standing here idle all day?' They[91] said to him, 'Because no one hired us.' He said to them, 'You also go into the vineyard, and whatever is right you will receive.' So when evening had come, the owner of the vineyard said to his steward, 'Call the laborers and give them their wages, beginning with the last to the first.' And when those came who were hired about the eleventh hour, they each received a denarius. But when the first came, they supposed that they would receive more; and they likewise received each a denarius. And when they had received it, they murmured against the landowner, saying, 'These last men have worked only one hour, and you made them equal to us who have borne the burden and the heat of the day.' But he answered one of them and said, 'Friend, I am doing you no wrong. Did you not agree with me for a denarius? Take what is yours and go your way. I wish to give to this last man the same as to you. Is it not lawful for me to do what I wish with my own things? Or is your eye evil because I am good?'"

18. "Suppose one of you has a servant who is plowing or looking after the sheep. When he comes in from the field, do you tell him to hurry along and eat his meal? Of

---

[91]*Realize*

course not! Instead, you say to him, 'Get my supper ready, then put on your apron and wait on me while I eat[92] and drink; after that you may have your meal.' The servant does not deserve thanks for obeying orders, does he? It is the same with you; when you have done all you have been told to do, say, 'We are ordinary servants; we have only done our duty.'"

19. "For it is just like a man about to go on a journey, who called his own slaves, and entrusted his possessions to them. And to one he gave five talents, to another, two, and to another, one, each according to his own ability; and he went on his journey. Immediately the one who had received the five talents went and traded with them, and gained five more talents. In the same manner the one who had received the two talents gained two more. But he who received the one talent went away and dug in the ground, and hid his master's money. Now after a long time the master of those slaves came and settled accounts with them. And the one who had received the five talents came up and brought five more talents, saying, 'Master, you entrusted five talents to me; see, I have gained five more talents.' His master said to him, 'Well done, good and faithful slave; you were faithful with a few things, I will put you in charge of many things; enter into the joy of your master.' The one also who had received the two talents came up and said,[93] 'Master, you entrusted to me two talents; see, I have gained two more talents.' His master said to him, 'Well done, good and faithful slave; you were faithful with a few things, I will put you in charge of many things; enter into the joy of your master.' And the one also who had received the one talent came up and said, 'Master, I knew you to be a hard man, reaping where you did not sow, and gathering where you scattered no seed. And I was afraid, and went away and hid your talent in the ground; see, you have what is yours.' But his master answered and said to him, 'You wicked, lazy slave. Take away the talent from him, and give it to the one who has

---

[92]*Steward*
[93]*Ordinary*

the ten talents.' For to everyone who has shall more be given, and he shall have an abundance; but from the one who does not have, even what he does have shall be taken away."

20. "And when the Son of Man comes in His glory, and all the holy angels with Him, then He will sit on the throne of His glory. All the nations will be gathered before Him, and He will separate them one from another, as a shepherd divides his sheep from the goats. And He will set the sheep on His right hand, but the goats on the left. Then the King will say to those on His right hand, 'Come, you blessed of My Father,[94] inherit the kingdom prepared for you from the foundation of the world: for I was hungry and you gave Me food; I was thirsty and you gave Me drink; I was a stranger and you took Me in; I was naked and you clothed Me; I was sick and you visited Me; I was in prison and you came to Me.' Then the righteous will answer Him, saying, 'Lord, when did we see You hungry and feed You, or thirsty and give You drink? When did we see You a stranger and take You in, or naked and clothe You? Or when did we see You sick, or in prison, and come to You?' And the King will answer and say to them, 'Assuredly, I say to you, inasmuch as you did it to one of the least of these My brethren, you did it to Me.' Then He will also say to those on the left hand, 'Depart from Me, you cursed, into the everlasting fire prepared for the devil and his angels: for I was hungry and you gave Me no food; I was thirsty and you gave Me no drink; I was a stranger and you did not take Me in, naked and you did not clothe Me, sick and in prison and you did not visit Me.' Then they also will answer Him, saying, 'Lord, when did we see You hungry or thirsty or a stranger or naked or sick or in prison, and did not minister to You?' Then He will answer them, saying, 'Assuredly, I say to you, inasmuch as you did not do it to one of the least of these, you did not do it to Me.'"[95]

---

[94] *Lazy*
[95] *Foundation*

21. "Who then is the faithful and wise servant, whom the master has put in charge of the servants in his household to give them their food at the proper time? It will be good for that servant whose master finds him doing so when he returns. But suppose that servant is wicked and says to himself, 'My master is staying away a long time,' and he then begins to beat his fellow servants and to eat and drink with drunkards. The master of that servant will come on a day when he does not expect him and at an hour he is not aware of. He will cut him to pieces and assign him a place with the hypocrites, where there will be weeping and gnashing of teeth."

+22. Now it came to pass, when Jesus had finished all these sayings, that He said to His disciples, "You know that tomorrow is the Passover, and the Son of Man will be delivered up to be crucified."

23.   Then the chief priests, the scribes, and the elders of the people assembled at the palace of the high priest, who was called Caiaphas, and plotted to take Jesus by trickery and kill Him. But they said, "Not during the feast, lest there be an uproar among the people."[96]

24. Then Jesus went with his disciples to a place called Gethsemane, and he said to them, "Sit here while I go over there and pray." He took with him Peter and the two sons of Zebedee. Grief and anguish came over him, and he said to them, "The sorrow in my heart is so great that it almost crushes me. Stay here and keep watch with me." He went a little farther on, threw himself face downward on the ground, and prayed, "My Father, if it is possible, take this cup of suffering from me! Yet not what I want, but what you want." Then he returned to the three disciples and found them asleep; and he said to Peter, "How is it that you three were not able to keep watch with me for even one hour? Keep watch and pray that you will not fall into temptation. The spirit is willing, but the flesh is weak."

---

[96] *Gnashing*

25. Once more Jesus went away and prayed, "My Father, if this cup of suffering cannot be taken away unless I drink it, your will be done." He returned once more and found the disciples asleep; they could not keep their eyes open.

26. Again Jesus left them, went away, lifted up His eyes to heaven, and said: "Father, the hour has come. Glorify Your Son, that Your Son[97] also may glorify You, as You have given Him authority over all flesh, that He should give eternal life to as many as You have given Him. And this is eternal life, that they may know You, the only true God. I have glorified You on the earth. I have finished the work which You have given Me to do. And now, O Father, glorify Me together with Yourself. Holy Father, keep through Your name those whom You have given Me, that they may be one as We are. I do not pray that You should take them out of the world, but that You should keep them from the evil one. They are not of the world, just as I am not of the world. Sanctify them by Your truth. As You sent Me into the world, I also have sent them into the world. O righteous Father! The world has not known You, but I have known You; and these have known that You sent Me. And I have declared to them Your name, and will declare it, that the love with which You loved Me may be in them, and I in them."

27. Then he returned to the disciples and said, "Are you still sleeping and resting? Look! The hour has come for the Son of Man to be handed over to the power of sinful men."[98]

---

[97] *Gethsemane*
[98] *Sanctify*

Ten....

1. And immediately, while He was still speaking, a great multitude with swords and clubs came from the chief priests and the scribes and the elders. Then Jesus spoke to the crowd, "Did you have to come with swords and clubs to capture me, as though I were an outlaw? Every day I sat down and taught in the Temple, and you did not arrest me. But this is your hour, and the power of darkness." Then they laid their hands on Him and took Him.

2. And they led Him away to Annas first, for he was the father-in-law of Caiaphas who was high priest that year. Then Annas sent him bound to Caiaphas the high priest. It was Caiaphas who had counseled the Jews that it was better that one man should die rather than the people.

3. The high priest then questioned Jesus about his disciples and his teaching.

4. Jesus answered him, "I have spoken openly to the world; I have always taught in synagogues and in the temple, where all Jews come together; I have said nothing secretly. Why do you ask me? Ask those who have[99] heard me, what I said to them; they know what I said."

5. When he had said this, one of the officers standing by struck Jesus with his hand, saying, "Is that how you answer the high priest?"

6. Jesus answered him, "If I have spoken wrongly, bear witness to the wrong; but if I have spoken rightly, why do you strike me?"

7. Now the chief priests and the whole Council kept trying to obtain testimony against Jesus to put Him to death; and they

---

[99] *Arrest*

were not finding any. For many were giving false testimony against Him, and yet their testimony was not consistent. And some stood up and began to give false testimony against Him, saying, "We heard Him say, 'I will destroy this temple made with hands, and in three days I will build another made without hands.'" And not even in this respect was their testimony consistent.

8. And the high priest stood up and came forward and questioned Jesus, saying, "Do You make no answer? What is it that these men are testifying against You?"[100]

9. But Jesus kept quiet and would not say a word.

10. Again the high priest was questioning Him, and saying to Him, "Are You the Christ, the Son of the Blessed One?"

11. And Jesus said, "I am."

12. Then the high priest tore his clothes, saying, "He has spoken blasphemy! What further need do we have of witnesses? Look, now you have heard His blasphemy! What do you think?"

13. They answered and said, "He is deserving of death."

14. Then they spat in His face and beat Him; and others struck Him with the palms of their hands, saying, "Prophesy to us, Christ! Who is the one who struck You?"

15. When morning came, all the chief priests and elders of the people took counsel against Jesus to put Him to death. And when they had bound Him, they led Him away and delivered

Him to Pontius Pilate the[101] governor.

16. Now Jesus stood before the governor. And the governor asked Him, saying, "Are You the King of the Jews?"

17. Jesus answered, "Are you saying this on your own initiative, or did others tell you about Me?"

18. Pilate answered, "I am not a Jew, am I? Your own nation and the chief priests delivered You up to me; what have You done?"

19. Jesus answered, "My kingdom is not of this world. If My kingdom were of this world, then My servants would be fighting, that I might not be delivered up to the Jews; but as it is, My kingdom is not of this realm."

20. Pilate therefore said to Him, "So You are a king?"

21. Jesus answered, "You say correctly that I am a king. For this I have been born, and for this I have come into the world, to bear witness to the truth. Everyone who is of the truth hears My voice."[102]

22. Pilate said to Him, "What is truth?" And when he had said this, he went out again to the Jews, and said to them, "I find no fault in Him at all."

23. Now at the feast the governor was accustomed to release for the multitude any one prisoner whom they wanted. And they were holding at that time a notorious prisoner, called Barabbas. When therefore they were gathered together, Pilate said to them, "Whom do you want me to release for you? Barabbas, or Jesus who is called Christ?" For he knew that because of envy they had delivered Him up.

---

[101] *Pontius*
[102] *Realm*

24. And while he was sitting on the judgment seat, his wife sent to him, saying, "Have nothing to do with that righteous Man; for last night I suffered greatly in a dream because of Him."

25. But the chief priests and the elders persuaded the multitudes to ask for Barabbas, and to put Jesus to death.

26. But the governor answered and said to them, "Which of the two do you want me to release for you?"[103]

27. And they said, "Barabbas."

28. Pilate said to them, "Then what shall I do with Jesus who is called Christ?"

29. They all said, "Let Him be crucified!"

30. And he said, "Why, what evil has He done?"

31. But they shouted all the more, "Crucify Him!"

32. And when Pilate saw that he was accomplishing nothing, but rather that a riot was starting, he took water and washed his hands in front of the multitude, saying, "I am innocent of this Man's blood."

33. And all the people answered and said, "His blood be on us and on our children!"

34. Then the soldiers of the governor took Jesus. And they stripped Him and put a scarlet robe on Him. When they had twisted a crown of[104] thorns, they put it on His head, and a reed in His right hand.

35. And they bowed the knee before Him and

---

[103] *Dream*
[104] *Barabbas*

mocked Him, saying, "Hail, King of the Jews!" Then they spat on Him, and took the reed and struck Him on the head.

36. Pilate then went out again, and said to them, "Behold, I am bringing Him out to you, that you may know that I find no fault in Him."

37. Then Jesus came out, wearing the crown of thorns and the purple robe. And Pilate said to them, "Behold the Man!"

38. When they had finished making fun of him, they took the robe off and put his own clothes back on him. Then they led him out to crucify him.

39. Now as they came out, they found a man of Cyrene, Simon by name. Him they compelled to bear His cross. And a great multitude of the people followed Him, and women who also mourned and lamented Him.

40. But Jesus, turning to them, said, "Daughters of Jerusalem, do not[105] weep for Me, but weep for yourselves and for your children. For indeed, the days are coming in which they will say, 'Blessed are the barren, the wombs that never bore, and the breasts which never nursed!'"

41. And when they had come to the place called Calvary, there they crucified Him. And an inscription also was written over Him in letters of Greek, Latin, and Hebrew: THIS IS THE KING OF THE JEWS.

42. Then two robbers were crucified with Him, one on the right and another on the left. And those who passed by blasphemed Him, wagging their heads.

43. Likewise the chief priests, also mocking with the scribes and elders, said, "He saved others; Himself He cannot save. If He is

---

[105]*Lamented*

the King of Israel, let Him now come down from the cross, and we will believe Him. He trusted in God; let Him deliver Him now if He will have Him; for He said, 'I am the Son of God.'" Even the robbers who were crucified with Him reviled Him with the same thing.

44. Then Jesus said, "Father, forgive them, for they do not know what they[106] do."

45. Now from the sixth hour until the ninth hour there was darkness over all the land. And about the ninth hour Jesus cried out with a loud voice, saying, "Eli, Eli, lama sabachthani?" that is, "My God, My God, why have You forsaken Me?"

46. After this, Jesus said, "I thirst!" Now a vessel full of sour wine was sitting there; and they filled a sponge with sour wine, put it on hyssop, and put it to His mouth. So when Jesus had received the sour wine, He said, "It is finished!" And bowing His head, He gave up His spirit.

47. Now when evening had come, there came a rich man from Arimathea, named Joseph, who himself had also become a disciple of Jesus. This man went to Pilate and asked for the body of Jesus. Then Pilate commanded the body to be given to him. And when Joseph had taken the body, he wrapped it in a clean linen cloth, and laid it in his new tomb which he had hewn out of the rock; and he rolled a large stone against the door of the tomb, and departed.[107]

48. On the next day, the chief priests and Pharisees gathered together to Pilate, saying, "Sir, we remember, while He was still alive, how that deceiver said, 'After three days I will rise.' Therefore, command that the tomb be made secure until the third day, lest His disciples come by night and

---

[106] *Calvary*
[107] *Sabachthani*

steal Him away, and say to the people, 'He has risen from the dead.' So the last deception will be worse than the first."

49. Pilate said to them, "You have a guard; go your way, make it as secure as you know how."

50. So they went and made the tomb secure, sealing the stone and setting the guard.

51. Now after the Sabbath, as the first day of the week began to dawn, Mary Magdalene and the other Mary came to see the tomb. And behold, there was a great earthquake; for an angel of the Lord descended from heaven, and came and rolled back the stone from the door, and sat on it. His countenance was like lightning, and his clothing as white as snow. And the guards shook for fear of him, and became like dead men.[108]

52. But the angel answered and said to the women, "Do not be afraid, for I know that you seek Jesus who was crucified. He is not here; for He is risen, as He said. Come, see the place where the Lord lay. And go quickly and tell His disciples that He is risen from the dead, and indeed He is going before you into Galilee; there you will see Him. Behold, I have told you."

53. So they departed quickly from the tomb with fear and great joy, and ran to bring His disciples word.

54. And as they went to tell His disciples, behold, Jesus met them, saying, "Rejoice!" And they came and held Him by the feet and worshiped Him. Then Jesus said to them, "Do not be afraid. Go and tell My brethren to go to Galilee, and there they will see Me."

55. Now while they were going, behold, some of the guard came into the city and reported to the chief priests all the things that had happened. When they had assembled with

---

[108]*Guard*

the elders and taken counsel, they gave a large sum of money to the soldiers, saying, "Tell them, 'His disciples came at night and stole Him away while we slept.' And if this comes to[109] the governor's ears, we will appease him and make you secure." So they took the money and did as they were instructed.

+56.   Then the disciples went away into Galilee, to the mountain which Jesus had appointed for them.

57.   And Jesus came and spoke to them, saying, "All authority has been given to Me in heaven and on earth. Go therefore and make disciples of all the nations, teaching them to observe all things that I have commanded you; and lo, I am with you always, even to the end of the age."[110]

---

[109] *Tomb*
[110] *Appointed*

Tenacity (T)

One

1. Grace and peace be multiplied to you in the knowledge of God and of Jesus our Lord, as His divine power has given to us all things that pertain to life and godliness, through the knowledge of Him who called us by glory and virtue, by which have been given to us exceedingly great and precious promises, that through these you may be partakers of the divine nature, having escaped the corruption that is in the world through lust.

2. But we have this treasure in earthen vessels, that the excellence of the power may be of God and not of us. We are hard pressed on every side, yet not crushed; we are perplexed, but not in despair; persecuted, but not forsaken; struck down, but not destroyed--always carrying about in the body the dying of the YAH-way Jesus, that the life of Jesus also may be manifested in our body. For we who live are always delivered to death for Jesus' sake, that the life of Jesus also may be manifested in our mortal flesh.

3. We must go through many hardships to enter the kingdom of God.[1]

4. My brethren, count it all joy when you fall into various trials, knowing that the testing of your faith produces patience.

5. Therefore we do not lose heart. Even though our outward man is perishing, yet the inward man is being renewed day by day.

---

[1] *Divine*

6.   This being so, I myself always strive to have a conscience without offense toward God and men.

7.   But in all things we commend ourselves as ministers of God: in much patience, in tribulations, in needs, in distresses, in stripes, in imprisonments, in tumults, in labors, in sleeplessness, in fastings; by purity, by knowledge, by longsuffering, by kindness, by the Holy Spirit, by sincere love, by the word of truth, by the power of God, by the armor of righteousness on the right hand and on the left.

+8.   Be strong in the YAH-way, and in the strength of His might. Put on the full armor of God, that you may be able to stand firm against the schemes of the devil. For our struggle is not against flesh and blood, but against the rulers, against the powers, against the world forces of this[2] darkness, against the spiritual forces of wickedness in the heavenly places. Stand firm therefore, having girded your loins with truth, and having put on the breastplate of righteousness, and having shod your feet with the preparation of the gospel of peace. And take the helmet of salvation, and the sword of the Spirit.

+9.   There is therefore now no condemnation to those who are in Christ Jesus, who do not walk according to the flesh, but according to the Spirit. For the law of the Spirit of life in Jesus YAH-way has made me free from the law of sin and death. For those who live according to the flesh set their mind on the things of the flesh, but those who live according to the Spirit, the things of the Spirit. For the mind set on the flesh is death, but the mind set on the Spirit is life and peace. If you live according to the flesh you will die; but if by the Spirit you put to death the deeds of the body, you will live. As many as are led by the Spirit of God, these are God's children.

10.   But now we have been delivered from the law,

---

[2]*Trials*

	having died to what we were held by, so that we should serve in the newness of the Spirit and not in the oldness of the letter.³
11.	Now God is the Spirit; and where the Spirit of the YAH-way is, there is liberty.
12.	In the past you did not know God, and so you were slaves of beings who are not gods. But now that you know God--or, I should say, now that God knows you--how is it that you want to turn back to those weak and pitiful ruling spirits? Why do you want to become their slaves all over again? You pay special attention to certain days, months, seasons, and years. Freedom is what we have--Christ has set us free! Stand, then, as free people, and do not allow yourselves to become slaves again.
+13.	Walk by the Spirit, and do not gratify the desires of the flesh.
14.	But when you follow your own wrong inclinations your lives will produce these evil results: impure thoughts, eagerness for lustful pleasure, idolatry, spiritism (that is, encouraging the activity of demons), hatred and fighting, jealousy and anger, constant effort to get the best for yourself, complaints and criticisms, the feeling that everyone else is wrong except those in your own little group--and there will be wrong doctrine, envy, murder, drunkenness, wild parties, and all⁴ that sort of thing. Let me tell you again as I have before, that anyone living that sort of life will not inherit the kingdom of God. But when the Holy Spirit controls our lives he will produce this kind of fruit in us: love, joy, peace, patience, kindness, goodness, faithfulness, gentleness and self-control. Against such things there is no law.

---

³*Newness*
⁴*Freedom*

15.	Now those who belong to Christ Jesus have crucified the flesh with its passions and desires. If we live by the Spirit, let us also walk by the Spirit. Let us not become boastful, challenging one another, envying one another.
16.	For he who sows to his flesh will of the flesh reap corruption, but he who sows to the Spirit will of the Spirit reap everlasting life. Therefore, as we have opportunity, let us do good to all.
+17.	Do not be foolish, but understand what the Lord's will is. Do not get drunk on wine, which leads to debauchery. Instead be filled with the Spirit.
18.	But if any of you lacks wisdom, he should pray to God, who will give it[5] to him; because God gives generously and graciously to all.
19.	Therefore, put away all filth and evil excess and humbly welcome the word that has been planted in you and is able to save your souls. Be doers of the word and not hearers only, deluding yourselves. For if anyone is a hearer of the word and not a doer, he is like a man who looks at his own face in a mirror. He sees himself, then goes off and promptly forgets what he looked like. But the one who peers into the perfect law of freedom and perseveres, and is not a hearer who forgets but a doer who acts, such a one shall be blessed in what he does.
20.	My brethren, show no partiality as you hold the faith of our Lord Jesus YAH-way, the Lord of glory. For if a man with gold rings and in fine clothing comes into your assembly, and a poor man in shabby clothing also comes in, and you pay attention to the one who wears the fine clothing and say, "Have a seat here, please," while you say to the poor man, "Stand there," or, "Sit at my feet," have you not made distinctions among yourselves, and become

---

[5] *Self-control*

judges with evil thoughts? Listen, my beloved brethren. Has not God chosen those who are poor in the world to be rich in faith and heirs of the kingdom which he has promised to[6] those who love him? But you have dishonored the poor man. Is it not the rich who oppress you, is it not they who drag you into court? If you really fulfil the royal law, according to the scripture, "You shall love your neighbor as yourself," you do well. But if you show partiality, you commit sin, and are convicted by the law as transgressors. For whoever keeps the whole law but fails in one point has become guilty of all of it. For he who said, "Do not commit adultery," said also, "Do not kill." If you do not commit adultery but do kill, you have become a transgressor of the law. So speak and so act as those who are to be judged under the law of liberty. For judgment is without mercy to one who has shown no mercy; yet mercy triumphs over judgment.

21. Above all, let your love for one another be intense, because love covers a multitude of sins.

+22. Therefore don't criticize and speak evil about each

---

[6] *Generously*

other. If you do, you will be fighting against God's law of loving one another, declaring it is wrong. But your job is not to decide whether this law is right or wrong, but to obey it. Only he who made the law can rightly judge among us. He alone decides to save us or destroy. So what right do you have to[7] judge or criticize others?

+23. You are inexcusable, O man, whoever you are who judge, for in whatever you judge another you condemn yourself; for you who judge practice the same things.

24. For it is not those who hear the law who are just in the sight of God; rather, those who observe the law will be justified. For when the Gentiles who do not have the law by nature observe the prescriptions of the law, they are a law for themselves even though they do not have the law.

25. Then let us no longer judge one another, but rather resolve never to put a stumbling block or hindrance in the way of a brother.

26. You Jews think all is well between yourselves and God because he gave his laws to you; you brag that you are his special friends. Yes, you know what he wants; you know right from wrong and favor the right because you have been taught his laws from earliest youth. You are so sure of the way to God that you could point it out to a blind man. You[8] think of yourselves as beacon lights, directing men who are lost in darkness to God. You think that you can guide the simple and teach even children the affairs of God, for you really know his laws, which are full of all knowledge and truth. Yes, you teach others--then why don't you teach yourselves? You tell others not to steal--do you steal? You say it is wrong to commit adultery-- do you do it? You say,

---

[7] *Fulfil*
[8] *Hindrance*

"Don't pray to idols," and then make money your god instead. You are so proud of knowing God's laws, but you dishonor him by breaking them. No wonder the Scriptures say that the world speaks evil of God because of you.

27. For he is not a Jew who is one outwardly, nor is that circumcision which is outward in the flesh; but he is a Jew who is one inwardly, and circumcision is that of the heart, in the Spirit, and not in the letter; whose praise is not from men but from God.

+28. Then what advantage has the Jew? Or what is the value of circumcision? Much in every way. To begin with, the Jews are entrusted with the oracles of God. What if some were unfaithful? Does their faithlessness nullify the faithfulness of God? By no means![9] Let God be true though every man be false, as it is written, "That thou mayest be justified in thy words, and prevail when thou art judged." But if our wickedness serves to show the justice of God, what shall we say? That God is unjust to inflict wrath on us? By no means! For then how could God judge the world? But if through my falsehood God's truthfulness abounds to his glory, why am I still being condemned as a sinner? And why not do evil that good may come?--as some people slanderously charge us with saying. Their condemnation is just. What then? Are we Jews any better off? No, not at all; for I have already charged that all men, both Jews and Greeks, are under the power of sin, as it is written: "None is righteous, no, not one; no one understands, no one seeks for God. All have turned aside, together they have gone wrong; no one does good, not even one." "Their throat is an open grave, they use their tongues to deceive." "The venom of asps is under their lips." "Their mouth is full of curses and bitterness." "Their feet are swift to shed blood, in their paths are ruin and misery, and the way of peace they do not know." "There is no fear

---

[9]*Beacon*

of God before their eyes." Now we know that whatever the law says it speaks to those who are under the law, so that every mouth may be stopped, and the whole world may be held accountable to God.[10]

29. Or is God the God of the Jews only? Is he not the God of the Gentiles also? Of course he is.

30. In truth I perceive that God shows no partiality. But in every nation whoever fears Him and works righteousness is accepted by Him.

31. Tribulation and anguish on every soul of man who does evil, of the Jew first and also of the Greek; but glory, honor, and peace to everyone who works what is good, to the Jew first and also to the Greek.

32. I urge you therefore, brothers, by the mercies of God, to offer your bodies as a living sacrifice, holy and pleasing to God, your spiritual worship. Do not conform yourself to this age but be transformed by the renewal of your mind, that you may discern what is the will of God, what is good and pleasing and perfect.

33. Sin must no longer rule in your mortal bodies, so that you obey the desires of your natural self. Nor must you surrender any part of yourselves to sin to be used for wicked purposes. Instead, give yourselves to God, as those who have been brought from death to life,[11] and surrender your whole being to him to be used for righteous purposes.

34. Thank God that though you once chose to be slaves of sin, now you have obeyed with all your heart the teaching to which God has committed you. And now you are free from your old master, sin; and you have become slaves to your new master,

---

[10] *Inflict*
[11] *Transformed*

	righteousness.
35.	Now to the King eternal, immortal, invisible, to God who alone is wise, be honor and glory forever and ever. Amen.

Two--Paul

1.	Blessed be the God and Father of our YAH-way Jesus Christ, the Father of mercies and God of all comfort, who comforts us in all our tribulation, that we may be able to comfort those who are in any trouble, with the comfort with which we ourselves are comforted by God.[12]
2.	And we have such trust through Christ toward God. Not that we are sufficient of ourselves to think of anything as being from ourselves, but our sufficiency is from God, who also made us sufficient as ministers of the new covenant, not of the letter but of the Spirit; for the letter kills, but the Spirit gives life.
3.	My brothers, if someone is caught in any kind of wrongdoing, those of you who are spiritual should set him right; but you must do it in a gentle way. And keep an eye on yourselves, so that you will not be tempted, too. Help carry one another's burdens, and in this way you will obey the law of the Lord. If someone thinks he is something when he really is nothing, he is only deceiving himself. Each one should judge his own conduct. If it is good, then he can be proud of what he himself has done, without having to compare it with what someone else has done. For everyone has to carry his own load.

---

[12]*Invisible*

4. Let no one despise your youth, but be an example to the believers in word, in conduct, in love, in spirit, in faith, in purity.

5. Flee the evil desires of youth, and pursue righteousness, faith, love and[13] peace, along with those who call on Christ out of a pure heart. Don't have anything to do with foolish and stupid arguments, because you know they produce quarrels. And the Lord's servant must not quarrel; instead, he must be kind to everyone, able to teach, not resentful. Those who oppose him he must gently instruct, in the hope that God will grant them repentance leading them to a knowledge of the truth.

+6. For the kingdom of God is righteousness and peace and joy in the Holy Spirit. He who serves the YAH-way in these things is acceptable to God and approved by men.

7. So then let us pursue the things which make for peace and the building up of one another.

8. We who are strong ought to bear with the failings of the weak and not to please ourselves. Each of us should please his neighbor for his good, to build him up.

9. Let us conduct ourselves properly, as people who live in the light of day--no orgies or drunkenness, no immorality or indecency, no fighting[14] or jealousy.

10. But put on the Lord Jesus Christ, and make no provision for the desires of the flesh.

11. May the God of steadfastness and encouragement grant you to live in such harmony with one another, in accord with Christ Jesus, that together you may

---

[13] *Believers*
[14] *Approved*

with one voice glorify the God and Father of our Lord Jesus Yah Yah.

12. Let love be genuine; hate what is evil, hold fast to what is good; love one another with brotherly affection; outdo one another in showing honor. Never flag in zeal, be aglow with the Spirit, serve the Lord. Rejoice in your hope, be patient in tribulation, be constant in prayer. Contribute to the needs of the saints, practice hospitality. Bless those who persecute you; bless and do not curse them. Rejoice with those who rejoice, weep with those who weep. Live in harmony with one another; do not be haughty, but associate with the lowly; never be conceited. Repay no one evil for evil, but take thought for what is noble in the sight of all. If possible, so far as it depends upon you, live peaceably[15] with all. Do not be overcome by evil, but overcome evil with good.

13. Be under obligation to no one--the only obligation you have is to love one another. Whoever does this has obeyed the Law. The commandments, "Do not commit adultery; do not commit murder; do not steal; do not desire what belongs to someone else"--all these, and any others besides, are summed up in the one command, "Love your neighbor as you love yourself." If you love someone, you will never do him wrong; to love, then, is to obey the whole Law.

14. May mercy, peace, and love be yours in abundance.

15. Paul lived for the next two years in his rented house and welcomed all who visited him, telling them with all boldness about the Kingdom of God and about the Lord Jesus YAH-way; and no one tried to stop him.[16]

---

[15] *Contribute*
[16] *Paul*

Three

1. To all who are in Rome, beloved of God, called to be saints: Grace to you and peace from God our Father and the Lord Jesus, the YAH-way.

2. I have been crucified with Christ; it is no longer I who live, but the YAH-way lives in me; and the life which I now live in the flesh I live by faith in the Son of God, who loved me and gave Himself for me.

3. The message of the cross is foolishness to those who are perishing, but to us who are being saved it is the power of God. For it is written: "I will destroy the wisdom of the wise, and the learning of the learned I will set aside." Where is the wise one? Where is the scribe? Where is the debater of this age? Has not God made the wisdom of the world foolish? For since in the wisdom of God the world did not come to know God through wisdom, it was the will of God through the foolishness of the proclamation to save those who have faith. For Jews demand signs and Greeks look for wisdom, but we proclaim the Lord crucified, a stumbling block to Jews and foolishness to Gentiles, but to those who are called, Jews and Greeks alike, YAH-way the power of God and the wisdom of God. For the foolishness of God is wiser than human wisdom,[17] and the weakness of God is stronger than human strength.

4. Let no one deceive himself. If anyone among you seems to be wise in this age, let him become a fool that he may become wise. For the wisdom of this world is foolishness with God. For it is written, "He catches the wise in their own craftiness."

---

[17] *Grace*

5. I tell you this, brethren: flesh and blood cannot inherit the kingdom of God, nor does the perishable inherit the imperishable. When the perishable puts on the imperishable, and the mortal puts on immortality, then shall come to pass the saying that is written: "Death is swallowed up in victory."

6. Do not love the world or the things in the world. If anyone loves the world, the love of the Father is not in him. For all that is in the world--the lust of the flesh, the lust of the eyes, and the pride of life--is not of the Father but is of the world. And the world is passing away, and the lust of it; but he who does the will of the YAH-way abides forever.[18]

7. The brother in lowly circumstances should take pride in his high standing, and the rich one in his lowliness, for he will pass away "like the flower of the field." For the sun comes up with its scorching heat and dries up the grass, its flower droops, and the beauty of its appearance vanishes. So will the rich person fade away in the midst of his pursuits.

8. But you, man of God, avoid all these things. Strive for righteousness, godliness, faith, love, endurance, and gentleness.

9. If anyone advocates a different doctrine, and does not agree with sound words, those of our YAH-way Jesus Christ, and with the doctrine conforming to godliness, he is conceited and understands nothing; but he has a morbid interest in controversial questions and disputes about words, out of which arise envy, strife, abusive language, evil suspicions, and constant friction between men of depraved mind and deprived of the truth, who suppose that godliness is a means of gain.

10. What did we bring into the world? Nothing! What can we take out of the world? Nothing! So then, if

---

[18]*Eyes*

we have food and clothes, that should[19] be enough for us. But those who want to get rich fall into temptation and are caught in the trap of many foolish and harmful desires, which pull them down to ruin and destruction. For the love of money is a source of all kinds of evil. Some have been so eager to have it that they have wandered away from the faith and have broken their hearts with many sorrows.

11. For godly sorrow produces repentance to salvation, not to be regretted; but the sorrow of the world produces death.

12. And we know that the Son of the YAH-way has come and has given us an understanding, that we may know Him who is true; and we are in Him who is true, in His Son Jesus the Lord. This is the true God and eternal life.

13. Beloved, I pray that in all respects you may prosper and be in good health.

14. Finally, brethren, farewell. Become complete. Be of good comfort, be of one mind, live in peace; and the God of love and peace will be with[20] you. Greet one another with a holy kiss. The grace of the Lord Jesus Christ, and the love of God, and the communion of the Holy Spirit be with you all. Amen.

---

[19] *Droops*
[20] *Pray*

Four--Paul

1. Paul, an apostle of Jesus Christ, by the commandment of God our Savior and the Lord Jesus Christ, our hope. Grace, mercy, and peace from God our Father and Jesus YAH-way our Lord.

2. If anyone thinks himself to be a prophet or spiritual, let him acknowledge that the things which I write to you are the commandments of the Lord.

3. If any of you has a dispute with another, dare he take it before the ungodly for judgment instead of before the saints? The very fact that you have lawsuits among you means you have been completely defeated already. Why not rather be wronged? Why not rather be[21] cheated? But instead, one brother goes to law against another--and this in front of unbelievers.

4. Now concerning the things of which you wrote to me: It is good for a man not to touch a woman.

5. It is God's will that you should be sanctified: that you should avoid sexual immorality; that each of you should learn to control his own body in a way that is holy and honorable. For God did not call us to be impure, but to live a holy life.

6. All things are lawful for me, but all things are not helpful. All things are lawful for me, but I will not be brought under the power of any.

7. Don't you realize that your bodies are actually parts and members of the Lord? So should I take part of God and join him to a prostitute? Never! And don't you know that if a man joins himself to a prostitute she becomes a part of him and he becomes a part of her? For YAH-way tells us in the Scripture that in

---

[21] *Communion*

	his sight the two become one person.[22]
8.	Do you not know that you are the temple of God and that the Spirit of God dwells in you?
9.	Dear brothers, don't be childish in your understanding of these things. Be innocent babies when it comes to planning evil, but be men of intelligence in understanding matters of this kind.
10.	Therefore let any one who thinks that he stands take heed lest he fall. No temptation has overtaken you that is not common to man.
11.	But since there is so much immorality, each man should have his own wife, and each woman her own husband. The husband should fulfill his marital duty to his wife, and likewise the wife to her husband. I say this as a concession, not as a command. I wish that all men were as I am. But each man has his own gift from God; one has this gift, another has that.
12.	(For who makes you different from anyone else? What do you have that you did not receive? And if you did receive it, why do you boast as though you did not?)[23]
13.	Now to the unmarried and the widows I say: It is good for them to stay unmarried, as I am. But if they cannot control themselves, they should marry, for it is better to marry than to burn with passion.
14.	But a married man concerns himself with worldly matters, because he wants to please his wife; and so he is pulled in two directions. An unmarried woman or a virgin concerns herself with the Lord's work, because she wants to be dedicated both in body and spirit; but a married woman concerns herself with

---

[22]*Body*
[23]*Different*

	worldly matters, because she wants to please her husband. So the man who marries does well, but the one who doesn't marry does even better.
15.	"We are allowed to do anything," so they say. That is true, but not everything is good. "We are allowed to do anything"--but not everything is helpful.
+16.	What is the outcome then, brethren? When you assemble, each one has a psalm, has a teaching, has a revelation, has an interpretation. Let all things be done for edification.[24]
+17.	Whether you eat or drink, or whatever you do, do all to the glory of God. Give no offense, either to the Jews or to the Greeks or to the church of the Lord, just as I also please all men in all things, not seeking my own profit, but the profit of many, that they may be saved.
18.	No one should be looking out for his own interests, but for the interests of others.
19.	For just preaching the Gospel isn't any special credit to me--I couldn't keep from preaching it if I wanted to. I would be utterly miserable. Woe unto me if I don't. Under this circumstance, what is my pay? It is the special joy I get from preaching the Good News without expense to anyone, never demanding my rights. And this has a real advantage: I am not bound to obey anyone just because he pays my salary; yet I have freely and happily become a servant of any and all so that I can win them to the Lord.
20.	Therefore, since we have this ministry, as we have received mercy, we do not lose heart. But we have renounced the hidden things of shame, not walking in craftiness nor handling the word of God

---

[24] *Edification*

deceitfully, but[25] by manifestation of the truth commending ourselves to every man's conscience in the sight of God. But even if our gospel is veiled, it is veiled to those who are perishing, whose minds the god of this age has blinded, who do not believe, lest the light of the gospel of the glory of the Lord, who is the image of the YAH-way, should shine on them. For it is the God who commanded light to shine out of darkness who has shone in our hearts to give the light of the knowledge of the glory of God in the face of Jesus Christ.

+21. We have spoken freely to you, and opened wide our hearts to you. We are not withholding our affection from you, but you are withholding yours from us.

22. Have I therefore become your enemy because I tell you the truth?

23. As a fair exchange--I speak as to my children--open wide your hearts also.

24. For the YAH-way has not given us a spirit of fear, but of power and of love and of a sound mind.[26]

25. Beware, brethren, lest there be in any of you an evil heart of unbelief in departing from the living God; but exhort one another daily, while it is called "Today," lest any of you be hardened through the deceitfulness of sin.

26. Do not be deceived: "Evil company corrupts good habits." Awake to righteousness, and do not sin.

27. But as for you, the Lord has poured out his Spirit on you. As long as his Spirit remains in you, you do not need anyone to teach you. For his Spirit teaches you about everything, and what he teaches is true, not false. Obey the Spirit's teaching, then, and remain

---

[25]*Church*
[26]*Commending*

in union with God.

+28. "For this is the covenant that I will make with the house of Israel: I will put My laws in their mind and write them on their hearts; and I will be their God, and they shall be My people. None of them shall teach his neighbor, and none his brother, saying, 'Know the YAH-way,' for all shall know Me, from the least of them to the greatest of them. For I will be merciful to their unrighteousness, and their sins and their[27] lawless deeds I will remember no more."

29. For you are all sons of God through faith in the YAH-way Jesus. For as many of you as were baptized into the Lord have put on the Lord. There is neither Jew nor Greek, there is neither slave nor free, there is neither male nor female; for you are all one in Christ Jesus.

30. But the Scripture has confined all under sin, that the promise by faith in Jesus Christ might be given to those who believe.

31. I write to you not because you do not know the truth but because you do, and because every lie is alien to the truth.

32. How great is the love the Father has lavished on us, that we should be called children of God!

33. And his commandment is this: we should believe in the name of his Son, Jesus Christ, and love one another just as he commanded us.

34. Dear friends, let us love one another, because love comes from God.[28] Whoever loves is a child of God and knows the YAH-way. Whoever does not love does not know God, for God is love. And God showed his love for us by sending his only Son into

---

[27] *Today*
[28] *Lavished*

the world, so that we might have life through him. This is what love is: it is not that we have loved God, but that he loved us and sent his Son to be the means by which our sins are forgiven. Dear friends, if this is how God loved us, then we should love one another. No one has ever seen God, but if we love one another, God lives in union with us, and his love is made perfect in us.

35. The YAH-way is love, and he who abides in love abides in God, and God in him.

36. There is no fear in love; but perfect love casts out fear, because fear involves torment. But he who fears has not been made perfect in love.

37. If someone says, "I love God," and hates his brother, he is a liar; for he who does not love his brother whom he has seen, how can he love God whom he has not seen? And this commandment we have from Him: that he who loves the Lord must love his brother also.[29]

38. But whoever has this world's goods, and sees his brother in need, and shuts up his heart from him, how does the love of YAH-way abide in him?

39. This is how we know what love is: Christ gave his life for us. We too, then, ought to give our lives for our brothers!

40. My little children, let us not love in word or in tongue, but in deed and in truth.

41. This is the message which we have heard from Him and declare to you, that God is light and in Him is no darkness at all. If we say that we have fellowship with Him, and walk in darkness, we lie and do not practice the truth. But if we walk in the light as He is in the light, we have fellowship with one another,

---

[29] *Sending*

and the blood of Jesus Christ His Son cleanses us from all sin. If we say that we have no sin, we deceive ourselves, and the truth is not in us. If we confess our sins, He is faithful and just to forgive us our sins and to cleanse us from all unrighteousness. If we say that we have not sinned, we make Him a liar, and His word is not in us.[30]

42. Anyone who claims to be in the light but hates his brother is still in the darkness.

43. He who loves his brother abides in the light. But he who hates his brother is in darkness and walks in darkness, and does not know where he is going, because the darkness has blinded his eyes.

44. Follow the way of love.

45. If I had the gift of being able to speak in other languages without learning them, and could speak in every language there is in all of heaven and earth, but didn't love others, I would only be making noise. If I had the gift of prophecy and knew all about what is going to happen in the future, knew everything about everything, but didn't love others, what good would it do? Even if I had the gift of faith so that I could speak to a mountain and make it move, I would still be worth nothing at all without love. If I gave everything I have to poor people, and if I were burned alive for preaching the Gospel but didn't love others, it would be of no value whatever. Love is very patient and kind, never jealous or envious, never boastful or proud, never haughty or selfish or[31] rude. Love does not demand its own way. It is not irritable or touchy. It does not hold grudges and it keeps no record of wrongs. It is never glad about injustice, but rejoices whenever truth wins out. If you love someone you will be loyal to him no matter what the cost. You will always believe in him,

---

[30]*Fellowship*
[31]*Prophecy*

always expect the best of him, and always stand your ground in defending him. All the special gifts and powers from God will someday come to an end, but love goes on forever. Someday prophecy, and speaking in unknown languages, and special knowledge--these gifts will disappear. Now we know so little, even with our special gifts, and the preaching of those most gifted is still so poor. But when we have been made perfect and complete, then the need for these inadequate special gifts will come to an end, and they will disappear. It's like this: when I was a child I spoke and thought and reasoned as a child does. But when I became a man my thoughts grew far beyond those of my childhood, and now I have put away the childish things. In the same way, we can see and understand only a little about God now, as if we were peering at his reflection in a poor mirror; but someday we are going to see him in his completeness, face to face. Now all that I know is hazy and blurred, but then I will see everything clearly, just as clearly as God sees into my heart right now. There are[32] three things that remain--faith, hope, and love--and the greatest of these is love.

+46. Dear brothers, you have been given freedom: not freedom to do wrong, but freedom to love and serve each other. For the whole Law can be summed up in this one command: "Love others as you love yourself."

47. But if you act like wild animals, hurting and harming each other, then watch out, or you will completely destroy one another.

48. Do not lie to one another, since you have put off the old man with his deeds, and have put on the new man, that you may be filled with the knowledge of His will in all wisdom and spiritual understanding; that you may have a walk worthy of the Lord, fully

---

[32]*Irritable*

pleasing Him, being fruitful in every good work and increasing in the knowledge of God; where there is neither Greek nor Jew, circumcised nor uncircumcised, barbarian, Scythian, slave nor free, but YAH-way is all and in all.

49. Therefore, as the elect of God, holy and beloved, put on tender mercies, kindness, humbleness of mind, meekness, longsuffering; bearing with[33] one another, and forgiving one another, if anyone has a complaint against another; even as Christ forgave you, so you also must do. But above all these things put on love, which is the bond of perfection. And let the peace of God rule in your hearts, to which also you were called in one body; and be thankful. Let the word of the Lord dwell in you richly in all wisdom. And whatever you do in word or deed, do all in the name of the YAH-way Jesus, giving thanks to God the Father through Him.

50. For do I now persuade men, or God? Or do I seek to please men? For if I still pleased men, I would not be a servant of Christ.

51. For to me, to live is the Lord, and to die is gain. But if I live on in the flesh, this will mean fruit from my labor; yet what I shall choose I cannot tell. For I am hard pressed between the two, having a desire to depart and be with Christ, which is far better. Nevertheless to remain in the flesh is more needful for you.

52. Do all things without murmuring and disputing, that you may become blameless and harmless, children of God without fault in the midst of a[34] crooked and perverse generation, among whom you shine as lights in the world.

53. Therefore if there is any consolation in YAH-way, if

---

[33]*New*
[34]*Thankful*

	any comfort of love, if any fellowship of the Spirit, if any affection and mercy, fulfill my joy by being like-minded, having the same love, being of one accord, of one mind. Let nothing be done through selfish ambition or conceit, but in lowliness of mind let each esteem others better than himself. Let each of you look out not only for his own interests, but also for the interests of others.
54.	Let your gentleness be evident to all. The Lord is near.
55.	Have no anxiety about anything, but in everything by prayer and supplication with thanksgiving let your requests be made known to God. And the peace of the YAH-way, which passes all understanding, will keep your hearts and your minds in the Lord Jesus. Finally, brethren, whatever is true, whatever is honorable, whatever is just, whatever is pure, whatever is lovely, whatever is gracious, if there is any excellence, if there is anything worthy of praise, think about these things.[35]
56.	And as many as walk according to this rule, peace and mercy be upon them. Brethren, the grace of our Christ Jesus the YAH-way be with your spirit. Amen.

Five--Peter

1.	Peter, an apostle of Jesus Christ. Blessed be the God and Father of our YAH-way Jesus Christ.
+2.	Be very careful how you live--not as unwise but as wise.

---

[35] *Anxiety*

3. For you were formerly darkness, but now you are light in the Lord; walk as children of light (for the fruit of the light consists in all goodness and righteousness and truth), trying to learn what is pleasing to Christ.

4. Stop lying to each other; tell the truth, for we are parts of each other and when we lie to each other we are hurting ourselves. If anyone is[36] stealing he must stop it and begin using those hands of his for honest work so he can give to others in need. Don't use bad language. Say only what is good and helpful to those you are talking to, and what will give them a blessing.

5. And be kind to one another, tenderhearted, forgiving one another, just as God in Christ also forgave you.

6. So I tell you this, and insist on it in the Lord, that you must no longer live as the Gentiles do, in the futility of their thinking. They are darkened in their understanding and separated from the life of God because of the ignorance that is in them due to the hardening of their hearts. Having lost all sensitivity, they have given themselves over to sensuality so as to indulge in every kind of impurity, with a continual lust for more. You, however, did not come to know the YAH-way that way. Surely you heard of him and were taught in him in accordance with the truth that is in Jesus. You were taught, with regard to your former way of life, to put off your old self, which is being corrupted by its deceitful desires; to be made new in the attitude of your minds; and to put on the new self, created to be like God in true righteousness and[37] holiness.

+7. And you He made alive, who were dead in

---

[36] *Formerly*
[37] *Sensitivity*

trespasses and sins, in which you once walked according to the course of this world, according to the prince of the power of the air, the spirit who now works in the sons of disobedience, among whom also we all once conducted ourselves in the lusts of our flesh, fulfilling the desires of the flesh and of the mind, and were by nature children of wrath.

8. I urge you, then--I who am a prisoner because I serve the Lord: live a life that measures up to the standard God set when he called you. Be always humble, gentle, and patient. Show your love by being tolerant with one another. Do your best to preserve the unity which the Spirit gives by means of the peace that binds you together. There is one body and one Spirit, just as there is one hope to which YAH-way has called you. There is one Lord, one faith, one baptism; there is one God and Father of all mankind, who is Lord of all, works through all, and is in all.

9. Each one of us has received a special gift in proportion to what God has given. Under his control all the different parts of the body fit together,[38] and the whole body is held together by every joint with which it is provided. So when each separate part works as it should, the whole body grows and builds itself up through love. And so we shall all come together to that oneness in our faith and in our knowledge of the Son of God; we shall become mature people, reaching to the very height of the Lord's full stature. Then we shall no longer be children, carried by the waves and blown about by every shifting wind of the teaching of deceitful men, who lead others into error by the tricks they invent. Instead, by speaking the truth in a spirit of love, we must grow up in every way to Christ, who is the head.

10. Be imitators of God, therefore, as dearly loved children, and live a life of love. But among you there must not be even a hint of sexual immorality, or of any kind of impurity, or of greed, because these are improper for YAH-way's holy people. Nor should there be obscenity, foolish talk or coarse joking,

---

[38] *Standard*

which are out of place, but rather thanksgiving.

11. For you know the grace of our Lord Jesus Christ, that though He was rich, yet for your sakes He became poor, that you through His poverty[39] might become rich. And in this I give my advice: It is to your advantage not only to be doing what you began and were desiring to do a year ago; but now you also must complete the doing of it; that as there was a readiness to desire it, so there also may be a completion out of what you have. For if there is first a willing mind, it is accepted according to what one has, and not according to what he does not have. For I do not mean that others should be eased and you burdened; but by an equality, that now at this time your abundance may supply their lack, that their abundance also may supply your lack--that there may be equality. As it is written, "He who gathered much had nothing left over, and he who gathered little had no lack."

12. Remember this: Whoever sows sparingly will also reap sparingly, and whoever sows generously will also reap generously. Each man should give what he has decided in his heart to give, not reluctantly or under compulsion, for God loves a cheerful giver.

13. Strive for peace with all men, and for the holiness without which no one will see the Lord.[40]

14. Continue to love each other with true brotherly love.

15. Do not neglect to show hospitality to strangers, for by this some have entertained angels without knowing it.

16. Let your character be free from the love of money, and be satisfied with what you have.

---

[39]*Oneness*
[40]*Reluctantly*

17. Let us throw off everything that hinders and the sin that so easily entangles, and let us run with perseverance the race marked out for us. Let us fix our eyes on Jesus, the author and perfecter of our faith.

18. Although He was a Son, He learned obedience from the things which He suffered. And having been made perfect, He became to all those who obey Him the source of eternal salvation.

19. For where a covenant is, there must of necessity be the death of the one who made it. For a covenant is valid only when men are dead, for it is never in force while the one who made it lives.[41]

+20. And being found in appearance as a man, Jesus humbled Himself by becoming obedient to the point of death, even death on a cross. Therefore also God highly exalted Him, and bestowed on Him the name which is above every name.

21. We then, as workers together with Him, also plead with you not to receive the grace of God in vain.

22. For though by this time you ought to be teachers, you have need again for someone to teach you the elementary principles of the oracles of God, and you have come to need milk and not solid food. For everyone who partakes only of milk is not accustomed to the word of righteousness, for he is a babe. But solid food is for the mature, who because of practice have their senses trained to discern good and evil.

23. If you are wise, live a life of steady goodness, so that only good deeds will pour forth. And if you don't brag about them, then you will be truly wise! And by all means don't brag about being wise and good if you are bitter and jealous and selfish; that is the

---

[41] *Valid*

worst sort of lie. For jealousy and selfishness are not God's kind of wisdom. Such things are[42] earthly, unspiritual, inspired by the devil. For wherever there is jealousy or selfish ambition, there will be disorder and every other kind of evil. But the wisdom that comes from heaven is first of all pure and full of quiet gentleness. Then it is peace-loving and courteous. It allows discussion and is willing to yield to others; it is full of mercy and good deeds. It is wholehearted and straightforward and sincere. And those who are peacemakers will plant seeds of peace and reap a harvest of goodness.

24. Where do all the fights and quarrels among you come from? They come from your desires for pleasure, which are constantly fighting within you. You want things, but you cannot have them, so you are ready to kill; you strongly desire things, but you cannot get them, so you quarrel and fight. You do not have what you want because you do not ask God for it. And when you ask, you do not receive it, because your motives are bad; you ask for things to use for your own pleasures.

25. You adulterous people, don't you know that friendship with the world is hatred toward the Lord? Anyone who chooses to be a friend of the world becomes an enemy of God.[43]

26. Or do you suppose it is in vain that the Scripture says, "YAH-way yearns jealously over the spirit which he has made to dwell in us"? Submit yourselves therefore to God. Resist the devil and he will flee from you.

27. Draw near to God and He will draw near to you. Cleanse your hands, you sinners; and purify your hearts, you double-minded.

---

[42] *Elementary*
[43] *Peace-loving*

28. Humble yourselves in the sight of the Christ, and Christ will lift you up.

29. Let him who boasts, boast of the YAH-way. For it is not the man who commends himself that is accepted, but the man whom the Lord commends.

30. For though we live in the world, we do not wage war as the world does.

31. We urge you, our brothers, to warn the idle, encourage the timid, help the weak, be patient with everyone. See that no one pays back wrong for wrong, but at all times make it your aim to do good to one another[44] and to all people. Do not restrain the Holy Spirit. Put all things to the test: keep what is good and avoid every kind of evil.

32. And may the Lord make you increase and abound in love to one another and to all.

33. But concerning brotherly love you have no need that I should write to you, for you yourselves are taught by the Lord to love one another. But we urge you, brethren, that you increase more and more; that you also aspire to lead a quiet life, to mind your own business, and to work with your own hands, as we commanded you, that you may walk properly toward those who are outside, and that you may lack nothing.

34. Let all things be done decently and in order.

35. For God is not the author of confusion but of peace.

36. We say this because we hear that there are some people among you who live lazy lives and who do nothing except meddle in other people's business. In the name of the Lord Jesus YAH-way we

---

[44]*Submit*

	command these[45] people and warn them to lead orderly lives and work to earn their own living.
+37.	The goal of our instruction is love from a pure heart and a good conscience and a sincere faith. For some men, straying from these things, have turned aside to fruitless discussion, wanting to be teachers of the Law, even though they do not understand either what they are saying or the matters about which they make confident assertions.
38.	These are murmurers, complainers, walking according to their own lusts; and they mouth great swelling words, flattering people to gain advantage.
39.	Beloved, do not imitate what is evil, but what is good. He who does good is of God, but he who does evil has not seen God.
+40.	And do not believe every spirit, but test the spirits, whether they are of Christ; because many false prophets have gone out into the world.
41.	In this the children of the YAH-way and the children of the devil are[46] manifest: Whoever does not practice righteousness is not of God, nor is he who does not love his brother. For this is the message that you heard from the beginning, that we should love one another.
42.	The way we may be sure that we know him is to keep his commandments. Whoever says, "I know him," but does not keep his commandments is a liar, and the truth is not in him.
43.	But whoever keeps His word, truly the love of God is perfected in him. By this we know that we are in Him. He who says he abides in Him ought himself also to walk just as He walked. Brethren, I write no

---

[45] *Aspire*
[46] *Assertions*

new commandment to you, but an old commandment which you have had from the beginning.

44. Whoever commits sin also commits lawlessness, and sin is lawlessness. Whoever abides in Him does not sin. Whoever sins has neither seen Him nor known Him.

45. Do not marvel, my brethren, if the world hates you.[47]

+46. Yet who will harm you if you are eager to do what is good?

47. For this is the will of God, that by doing good you may put to silence the ignorance of foolish men--as free, yet not using your liberty as a cloak for vice, but as servants of God.

48. We know that we have passed from death to life, because we love the brethren. He who does not love his brother abides in death. Whoever hates his brother is a murderer, and you know that no murderer has eternal life abiding in him.

49. Finally, all of you, be of one mind, sympathetic, loving toward one another, compassionate, humble. Do not return evil for evil, or insult for insult; but, on the contrary, a blessing.

50. Beloved, I beg you as sojourners and pilgrims, abstain from fleshly lusts which war against the soul.

+51. And since you have purified your souls in obeying the truth through the Spirit in sincere love of the brethren, love one another fervently[48] with a pure heart, having been born again, not of corruptible seed but incorruptible, through the word of God which lives and abides forever.

---

[47] *Perfected*
[48] *Insult*

52.	Greet one another with a kiss of love. Peace to all of you who are in Christ.

Six....

1.	God, who at various times and in different ways spoke in time past to the fathers by the prophets, has in these last days spoken to us by His Son.

2.	Therefore we must give the more earnest heed to the things we have heard, lest we drift away.

3.	Not many of you should presume to be teachers, my brothers, because you know that we who teach will be judged more strictly. We all stumble in many ways. If anyone is never at fault in what he says, he[49] is a perfect man, able to keep his whole body in check. When we put bits into the mouths of horses to make them obey us, we can turn the whole animal. Or take ships as an example. Although they are so large and are driven by strong winds, they are steered by a very small rudder wherever the pilot wants to go. Likewise the tongue is a small part of the body, but it makes great boasts. Consider what a great forest is set on fire by a small spark. The tongue also is a fire, a world of evil among the parts of the body. It corrupts the whole person, sets the whole course of his life on fire, and is itself set on fire by hell. All kinds of animals, birds, reptiles and creatures of the sea are being tamed and have been tamed by man, but no man can tame the tongue. It is a restless evil, full of deadly poison. With the tongue we praise our Lord and Father, and with it we curse men, who have been made in God's likeness. Out of the same mouth come praise and

---

[49]*Kiss*

cursing. My brothers, this should not be. Can both fresh water and salt water flow from the same spring? My brothers, can a fig tree bear olives, or a grapevine bear figs? Neither can a salt spring produce fresh water.

4. Know this, my dear brothers: everyone should be quick to hear, slow to speak, slow to wrath, for the wrath of a man does not accomplish the[50] righteousness of God.

5. If anyone thinks he is religious and does not bridle his tongue but deceives his heart, his religion is vain.

6. Come now, you who say, "Today or tomorrow we will go to such and such a city, spend a year there, buy and sell, and make a profit"; whereas you do not know what will happen tomorrow. For what is your life? It is even a vapor that appears for a little time and then vanishes away. Instead you ought to say, "If the Lord wills, we shall live and do this or that." But now you boast in your arrogance. All such boasting is evil.

7. Come now, you rich, weep and howl for the miseries that are coming upon you. Your riches have rotted and your garments are moth-eaten. Your gold and silver have rusted, and their rust will be evidence against you and will eat your flesh like fire.

8. Look! The wages you failed to pay the workmen who mowed your fields are crying out against you. The cries of the harvesters have[51] reached the ears of the Lord Almighty.

9. You have spent your years here on earth having fun, satisfying your every whim, and now your fat hearts are ready for the slaughter.

---

[50] *Horses*
[51] *Howl*

10. You have condemned and put to death the righteous man; he does not resist you.

11. Brethren, if anyone among you wanders from the truth, and someone turns him back, let him know that he who turns a sinner from the error of his way will save a soul from death and cover a multitude of sins.

12. But above all, my brethren, do not swear, either by heaven or by earth or with any other oath. But let your "Yes" be "Yes," and your "No," "No," lest you fall into judgment.

13. Dear brothers, what's the use of saying that you have faith and are Christians if you aren't proving it by helping others? Will that kind of faith save anyone? If you have a friend who is in need of food and clothing, and you say to him, "Well, good-bye and God bless you; stay[52] warm and eat hearty," and then don't give him clothes or food, what good does that do? So you see, it isn't enough just to have faith. You must also do good to prove that you have it. Faith that doesn't show itself by good works is no faith at all--it is dead and useless.

14. But someone may well say, "You have faith, and I have works; show me your faith without the works, and I will show you my faith by my works."

15. Just as the body is dead when there is no spirit in it, so faith is dead if it is not the kind that results in good deeds.

16. What God the Father considers to be pure and genuine religion is this: to take care of orphans and widows in their suffering and to keep oneself from being corrupted by the world.

---

[52] *W him*

+17. YAH-way has revealed his grace for the salvation of all mankind; instructing us to deny ungodliness and worldly desires and to live sensibly, righteously and godly in the present age.[53]

18. For bodily exercise profits a little, but godliness is profitable for all things.

+19. For this very reason, giving all diligence, add to your faith virtue, to virtue knowledge, to knowledge self-control, to self-control perseverance, to perseverance godliness, to godliness brotherly kindness, and to brotherly kindness love. For if these things are yours and abound, you will be neither barren nor unfruitful in the knowledge of our YAH-way Jesus the Lord. But he who lacks these things is shortsighted, even to blindness, and has forgotten that he was cleansed from his old sins.

20. Examine yourselves, to see whether you are holding to your faith. Test yourselves. Do you not realize that Jesus Christ is in you?--unless indeed you fail to meet the test!

21. Therefore, brethren, be even more diligent to make your calling and election sure, for if you do these things you will never stumble.

22. That which we have seen and heard we declare to you, that you also may have fellowship with us; and truly our fellowship is with the[54] Father and with His Son Jesus the Lord. And these things we write to you that your joy may be full.

23. Watch, stand fast in the faith, be brave, be strong. Let all that you do be done with love. My love be with you all in the YAH-way Jesus. Amen.[55]

---

[53]*Orphans*
[54]*Shortsighted*
[55]*Father*

Works Cited

Vivacity (Viva City)

accept	www.lulu.com/shop/mike-marty/accept/ebook/product-23768425.html (Retrieved 4/23/25)
accuse	https://www.amazon.com/dp/B076BBD3F7 (Retrieved 4/23/25)
alabaster	www.lulu.com/shop/mike-marty/alabaster/ebook/product-23771186.html (Retrieved 4/23/25)
alms	https://www.lulu.com/shop/mike-marty/alms/ebook/product-23771214.html (Retrieved 4/23/25)
Andrew	www.lulu.com/shop/mike-marty/andrew/ebook/product-23773897.html (Retrieved 4/23/25)
appointed	www.lulu.com/shop/mike-marty/appointed/ebook/product-23774948.html (Retrieved 4/23/25)
arrest	www.lulu.com/shop/mike-marty/arrest/ebook/product-23777568.html (Retrieved 4/23/25)
Barabbas	https://www.amazon.com/dp/B0768V8G61 (Retrieved 4/23/25)
barn	https://www.lulu.com/shop/mike-marty/barn/ebook/product-23762021.html (Retrieved 4/23/25)
bondage	https://www.amazon.com/dp/B077LTG22S (Retrieved 4/23/25)
borrow	www.lulu.com/shop/mike-marty/borrow/ebook/product-23756819.html (Retrieved 4/23/25)
brave	www.lulu.com/shop/mike-marty/brave/ebook/product-23755140.html (Retrieved 4/23/25)
brothers	www.lulu.com/shop/mike-marty/brothers/ebook/product-23752691.html (Retrieved 4/23/25)
build	www.lulu.com/shop/mike-marty/build/ebook/product-23752673.html (Retrieved 4/23/25)
Caesar	www.lulu.com/shop/mike-marty/caesar/ebook/product-23752662.html (Retrieved 4/23/25)
calloused	www.lulu.com/shop/mike-marty/calloused/ebook/product-23750106.html (Retrieved 4/23/25)
Calvary	https://www.amazon.com/dp/B0768B3B1X (Retrieved 4/23/25)
chief	https://www.amazon.com/dp/B076PN9DJC (Retrieved 4/23/25)
confessed	www.lulu.com/shop/mike-marty/confessed/ebook/product-23745994.html (Retrieved 4/23/25)
constricted	www.lulu.com/shop/mike-marty/constricted/ebook/product-23743477.html (Retrieved 4/23/25)
Counselor	www.lulu.com/shop/mike-marty/counselor/ebook/product-23741578.html (Retrieved 4/23/25)
cross-examine	https://www.amazon.com/dp/B077MFTK6C (Retrieved 4/23/25)
David	https://www.amazon.com/dp/B0767HRNYC (Retrieved 4/23/25)
debtors	https://www.amazon.com/dp/B0768X1W7M (Retrieved 4/23/25)
decaying	www.lulu.com/shop/mike-marty/decaying/ebook/product-23739599.html (Retrieved 4/23/25)
demon	www.lulu.com/shop/mike-marty/demon/ebook/product-23737092.html (Retrieved 4/23/25)
dispute	www.lulu.com/shop/mike-marty/dispute/ebook/product-23735187.html (Retrieved 4/23/25)
ditches	www.lulu.com/shop/mike-marty/ditches/ebook/product-23732818.html (Retrieved 4/23/25)
dragged	www.lulu.com/shop/mike-marty/dragged/ebook/product-23730240.html (Retrieved 4/23/25)
dream	https://www.amazon.com/dp/B077NY9FFS (Retrieved 4/23/25)
excused	https://www.amazon.com/dp/B077PR43F6 (Retrieved 4/23/25)
farewell	www.lulu.com/shop/mike-marty/farewell/ebook/product-23720294.html (Retrieved 4/23/25)
filled	https://www.amazon.com/dp/B076FF1PCD (Retrieved 4/23/25)
flickering	www.lulu.com/shop/mike-marty/flickering/ebook/product-23717560.html (Retrieved 4/23/25)
fog	https://www.lulu.com/shop/mike-marty/fog/ebook/product-23674032.html (Retrieved 4/23/25)
forefathers	www.lulu.com/shop/mike-marty/forefathers/ebook/product-23715829.html (Retrieved 4/23/25)
forty	www.lulu.com/shop/mike-marty/forty/ebook/product-23713284.html (Retrieved 4/23/25)
foundation	https://www.amazon.com/dp/B077QXTHDZ (Retrieved 4/23/25)
Gethsemane	www.lulu.com/shop/mike-marty/gethsemane/ebook/product-23710184.html (Retrieved 4/23/25)
gnashing	www.lulu.com/shop/mike-marty/gnashing/ebook/product-23707594.html (Retrieved 4/23/25)
God	https://www.amazon.com/dp/B076GW947Y (Retrieved 4/23/25)
good-for-nothing	https://www.lulu.com/shop/mike-marty/good-for-nothing/ebook/product-23707579.html (Retrieved 4/23/25)
gospel	https://www.amazon.com/dp/B076NFW5Y7 (Retrieved 4/23/25)
guard	https://www.amazon.com/dp/B076VQSR1J (Retrieved 4/23/25)
hardhearted	www.lulu.com/shop/mike-marty/hardhearted/ebook/product-23705299.html (Retrieved 4/23/25)

hero	https://www.lulu.com/shop/mike-marty/hero/ebook/product-23701505.html (Retrieved 4/23/25)
household	www.lulu.com/shop/mike-marty/household/ebook/product-23697409.html (Retrieved 4/23/25)
hypocrisy	www.lulu.com/shop/mike-marty/hypocrisy/ebook/product-23695573.html (Retrieved 4/23/25)
important	www.lulu.com/shop/mike-marty/important/ebook/product-23692903.html (Retrieved 4/23/25)
innkeeper	https://www.amazon.com/dp/B0769ZC4HS (Retrieved 4/23/25)
invited	www.lulu.com/shop/mike-marty/invited/ebook/product-23688874.html (Retrieved 4/23/25)
Iscariot	www.lulu.com/shop/mike-marty/iscariot/ebook/product-23686989.html (Retrieved 4/23/25)
jail	https://www.lulu.com/shop/mike-marty/jail/ebook/product-23685265.html (Retrieved 4/23/25)
James	www.lulu.com/shop/mike-marty/james/ebook/product-23685261.html (Retrieved 4/23/25)
Jesus	https://www.amazon.com/dp/B0765ZQZ8L (Retrieved 4/23/25)
lamented	www.lulu.com/shop/mike-marty/lamented/ebook/product-23685253.html (Retrieved 4/23/25)
lawyer	https://www.amazon.com/dp/B076B6DC3T (Retrieved 4/23/25)
lazy	https://www.amazon.com/dp/B0765VJHQN (Retrieved 4/23/25)
lightning	www.lulu.com/shop/mike-marty/lightning/ebook/product-23680021.html (Retrieved 4/23/25)
lucky	www.lulu.com/shop/mike-marty/lucky/ebook/product-23678726.html (Retrieved 4/23/25)
manager	www.lulu.com/shop/mike-marty/manager/ebook/product-23678710.html (Retrieved 4/23/25)
manna	www.lulu.com/shop/mike-marty/manna/ebook/product-23676711.html (Retrieved 4/23/25)
Martha	www.lulu.com/shop/mike-marty/martha/ebook/product-23676687.html (Retrieved 4/23/25)
Mary	https://www.amazon.com/dp/B0768WF5Z1 (Retrieved 4/23/25)
mercy	https://www.amazon.com/dp/B076ZMJ9XY (Retrieved 4/23/25)
messenger	www.lulu.com/shop/mike-marty/messenger/ebook/product-23674043.html (Retrieved 4/23/25)
millstone	www.lulu.com/shop/mike-marty/millstone/ebook/product-23817657.html (Retrieved 4/23/25)
moneychangers	https://www.amazon.com/dp/B0768VZRLF (Retrieved 4/23/25)
needle	www.lulu.com/shop/mike-marty/needle/ebook/product-23670153.html (Retrieved 4/23/25)
Nicodemus	www.lulu.com/shop/mike-marty/nicodemus/ebook/product-23670134.html (Retrieved 4/23/25)
ninety-nine	www.lulu.com/shop/mike-marty/ninety-nine/ebook/product-23668033.html (Retrieved 4/23/25)
offended	https://www.amazon.com/dp/B0765KHBK5 (Retrieved 4/23/25)
ordinary	www.lulu.com/shop/mike-marty/ordinary/ebook/product-23667003.html (Retrieved 4/23/25)
owner	www.lulu.com/shop/mike-marty/owner/ebook/product-23664547.html (Retrieved 4/23/25)
Passover	www.lulu.com/shop/mike-marty/passover/ebook/product-23661928.html (Retrieved 4/23/25)
Pharisee	www.lulu.com/shop/mike-marty/pharisee/ebook/product-23658782.html (Retrieved 4/23/25)
places	www.lulu.com/shop/mike-marty/places/ebook/product-23655817.html (Retrieved 4/23/25)
pluck	https://www.amazon.com/dp/B077SDGFKS (Retrieved 4/23/25)
Pontius	www.lulu.com/shop/mike-marty/pontius/ebook/product-23655788.html (Retrieved 4/23/25)
pretenders	www.lulu.com/shop/mike-marty/pretenders/ebook/product-23654026.html (Retrieved 4/23/25)
questioned	https://www.amazon.com/dp/B0765NB3VR (Retrieved 4/25/25)
realize	www.lulu.com/shop/mike-marty/realize/ebook/product-23649814.html (Retrieved 4/25/25)
realm	https://www.amazon.com/dp/B0768B2WQ4 (Retrieved 4/25/25)
resources	https://www.amazon.com/dp/B0784RHGLM (Retrieved 4/25/25)
sabachthani	https://www.amazon.com/dp/B0763HBBGP (Retrieved 4/25/25)
Samaria	www.lulu.com/shop/mike-marty/samaria/ebook/product-23641249.html (Retrieved 4/25/25)
sanctify	www.lulu.com/shop/mike-marty/sanctify/ebook/product-23641237.html (Retrieved 4/25/25)
sawdust	www.lulu.com/shop/mike-marty/sawdust/ebook/product-23638379.html (Retrieved 4/25/25)
scatter	www.lulu.com/shop/mike-marty/scatter/ebook/product-23638363.html (Retrieved 4/25/25)
scorched	www.lulu.com/shop/mike-marty/scorched/ebook/product-23638324.html (Retrieved 4/25/25)
scoundrels	https://www.amazon.com/dp/B076Y78JWM (Retrieved 4/25/25)
scribes	www.lulu.com/shop/mike-marty/scribes/ebook/product-23635508.html (Retrieved 4/25/25)
Scriptures	https://www.amazon.com/dp/B0763LHB9K (Retrieved 4/25/25)
sexual	www.lulu.com/shop/mike-marty/sexual/ebook/product-23630988.html (Retrieved 4/25/25)
started	www.lulu.com/shop/mike-marty/started/ebook/product-23626493.html (Retrieved 4/25/25)

steward	www.lulu.com/shop/mike-marty/steward/ebook/product-23623713.html (Retrieved 4/25/25)
teachers	www.lulu.com/shop/mike-marty/teachers/ebook/product-23619903.html (Retrieved 4/25/25)
thirst	https://www.amazon.com/dp/B076HDWZL8 (Retrieved 4/25/25)
thirtyfold	www.lulu.com/shop/mike-marty/thirtyfold/ebook/product-23614227.html (Retrieved 4/25/25)
tomb	https://www.amazon.com/dp/B077V5Q2FG (Retrieved 4/25/25)
tradition	www.lulu.com/shop/mike-marty/tradition/ebook/product-23613406.html (Retrieved 4/25/25)
twelve	www.lulu.com/shop/mike-marty/twelve/ebook/product-23605867.html (Retrieved 4/25/25)
urged	https://www.amazon.com/dp/B076JGPPK1 (Retrieved 4/25/25)
verdict	www.lulu.com/shop/mike-marty/verdict/ebook/product-23600404.html (Retrieved 4/25/25)
washbasin	www.lulu.com/shop/mike-marty/washbasin/ebook/product-23598928.html (Retrieved 4/25/25)
where	www.lulu.com/shop/mike-marty/where/ebook/product-23595828.html (Retrieved 4/25/25)
wither	https://www.amazon.com/dp/B0763J71FZ (Retrieved 4/25/25)
worshiped	https://www.amazon.com/dp/B077WHCX6V (Retrieved 4/25/25)
Yes	https://www.lulu.com/shop/mike-marty/yes/ebook/product-23592765.html (Retrieved 4/25/25)
younger	www.lulu.com/shop/mike-marty/younger/ebook/product-23592400.html (Retrieved 4/25/25)

Tenacity

anxiety	www.lulu.com/shop/mike-marty/anxiety/ebook/product-23774974.html (Retrieved 4/25/25)
approved	www.lulu.com/shop/mike-marty/approved/ebook/product-23777548.html (Retrieved 4/25/25)
aspire	www.lulu.com/shop/mike-marty/aspire/ebook/product-23764662.html (Retrieved 4/25/25)
assertions	www.lulu.com/shop/mike-marty/assertions/ebook/product-23764651.html (Retrieved 4/25/25)
beacon	www.lulu.com/shop/mike-marty/beacon/ebook/product-23760963.html (Retrieved 4/25/25)
believers	www.lulu.com/shop/mike-marty/believers/ebook/product-23760938.html (Retrieved 4/25/25)
body	https://www.lulu.com/shop/mike-marty/body/ebook/product-23758426.html (Retrieved 4/25/25)
church	www.lulu.com/shop/mike-marty/church/ebook/product-23750037.html (Retrieved 4/25/25)
commending	www.lulu.com/shop/mike-marty/commending/ebook/product-23749195.html (Retrieved 4/25/25)
communion	www.lulu.com/shop/mike-marty/communion/ebook/product-23749183.html (Retrieved 4/25/25)
contribute	www.lulu.com/shop/mike-marty/contribute/ebook/product-23743452.html (Retrieved 4/25/25)
different	www.lulu.com/shop/mike-marty/different/ebook/product-23737028.html (Retrieved 4/25/25)
divine	www.lulu.com/shop/mike-marty/divine/ebook/product-23732789.html (Retrieved 4/25/25)
droops	www.lulu.com/shop/mike-marty/droops/ebook/product-23730226.html (Retrieved 4/25/25)
edification	www.lulu.com/shop/mike-marty/edification/ebook/product-23728484.html (Retrieved 4/25/25)
elementary	www.lulu.com/shop/mike-marty/elementary/ebook/product-23726271.html (Retrieved 4/25/25)
eyes	https://www.lulu.com/shop/mike-marty/eyes/ebook/product-23720286.html (Retrieved 4/25/25)
Father	https://www.amazon.com/dp/B075748LXX (Retrieved 4/25/25)
fellowship	www.lulu.com/shop/mike-marty/fellowship/ebook/product-23717580.html (Retrieved 4/25/25)
formerly	www.lulu.com/shop/mike-marty/formerly/ebook/product-23713300.html (Retrieved 4/25/25)
freedom	www.lulu.com/shop/mike-marty/freedom/ebook/product-23713264.html (Retrieved 4/25/25)
fulfil	www.lulu.com/shop/mike-marty/fulfil/ebook/product-23711346.html (Retrieved 4/25/25)
generously	www.lulu.com/shop/mike-marty/generously/ebook/product-23710141.html (Retrieved 4/25/25)
grace	www.lulu.com/shop/mike-marty/grace/ebook/product-23707560.html (Retrieved 4/25/25)
hindrance	www.lulu.com/shop/mike-marty/hindrance/ebook/product-23701471.html (Retrieved 4/25/25)
horses	www.lulu.com/shop/mike-marty/horses/ebook/product-23697416.html (Retrieved 4/25/25)
howl	https://www.lulu.com/shop/mike-marty/howl/ebook/product-23697407.html (Retrieved 4/25/25)
inflict	https://www.amazon.com/dp/B0757R6TLP (Retrieved 4/25/25)
insult	www.lulu.com/shop/mike-marty/insult/ebook/product-23691498.html (Retrieved 4/25/25)
invisible	www.lulu.com/shop/mike-marty/invisible/ebook/product-23688879.html (Retrieved 4/25/25)
irritable	www.lulu.com/shop/mike-marty/irritable/ebook/product-23688854.html (Retrieved 4/25/25)
kiss	https://www.lulu.com/shop/mike-marty/kiss/ebook/product-23685257.html (Retrieved 4/25/25)
lavished	www.lulu.com/shop/mike-marty/lavished/ebook/product-23683329.html (Retrieved 4/25/25)
new	https://www.lulu.com/shop/mike-marty/new/ebook/product-23670174.html (Retrieved 4/25/25)
newness	www.lulu.com/shop/mike-marty/newness/ebook/product-23670111.html (Retrieved 4/25/25)
oneness	www.lulu.com/shop/mike-marty/oneness/ebook/product-23667991.html (Retrieved 4/25/25)
orphans	www.lulu.com/shop/mike-marty/orphans/ebook/product-23666962.html (Retrieved 4/25/25)
Paul	https://www.lulu.com/shop/mike-marty/paul/ebook/product-23661889.html (Retrieved 4/25/25)
peace-loving	www.lulu.com/shop/mike-marty/peace-loving/ebook/product-23661137.html (Retrieved 4/25/25)
perfected	www.lulu.com/shop/mike-marty/perfected/ebook/product-23661108.html (Retrieved 4/25/25)
pray	https://www.lulu.com/shop/mike-marty/pray/ebook/product-23654038.html (Retrieved 4/25/25)
prophecy	www.lulu.com/shop/mike-marty/prophecy/ebook/product-23652373.html (Retrieved 4/25/25)
reluctantly	www.lulu.com/shop/mike-marty/reluctantly/ebook/product-23648217.html (Retrieved 4/25/25)
self-control	www.lulu.com/shop/mike-marty/self-control/ebook/product-23635454.html (Retrieved 4/25/25)
sending	www.lulu.com/shop/mike-marty/sending/ebook/product-23633438.html (Retrieved 4/25/25)
sensitivity	www.lulu.com/shop/mike-marty/sensitivity/ebook/product-23633417.html (Retrieved 4/25/25)
shortsighted	www.lulu.com/shop/mike-marty/shortsighted/ebook/product-23630962.html (Retrieved 4/25/25)
standard	www.lulu.com/shop/mike-marty/standard/ebook/product-23626508.html (Retrieved 4/25/25)

submit	www.lulu.com/shop/mike-marty/submit/ebook/product-23619948.html (Retrieved 5/1/25)
thankful	https://www.amazon.com/dp/B0756NQT6F (Retrieved 5/1/25)
today	https://www.lulu.com/shop/mike-marty/today/ebook/product-23614215.html (Retrieved 5/1/25)
transformed	www.lulu.com/shop/mike-marty/transformed/ebook/product-23613382.html (Retrieved 5/1/25)
trials	https://www.lulu.com/shop/mike-marty/trials/ebook/product-23606914.html (Retrieved 5/1/25)
valid	https://www.lulu.com/shop/mike-marty/valid/ebook/product-23603088.html (Retrieved 5/1/25)
whim	https://www.lulu.com/shop/mike-marty/whim/ebook/product-23595795.html (Retrieved 5/1/25)

www.ingramcontent.com/pod-product-compliance
Lightning Source LLC
Chambersburg PA
CBHW052032030426
42337CB00027B/4973